SHARING

YOUR GOOD

IDEAS

★ ★ ★ ★

A WORKSHOP FACILITATOR'S HANDBOOK

Peggy A. Sharp

Heinemann • Portsmouth, NH

Heinemann
A division of Reed Publishing (USA) Inc.
361 Hanover Street
Portsmouth, NH 03801-3912
Offices and agents throughout the world

Library of Congress Cataloging-in-Publication Data

Sharp, Peggy Agostino.
    Sharing your good ideas : a workshop facilitator's handbook / by Peggy A. Sharp.
        p. cm
    Includes bibliographical references (p.).
    ISBN 0-435-08783-5
        1. Teachers—In-service training—Planning—Handbooks, manuals, etc. 2. Education—
Congresses—Planning—Handbooks, manuals, etc.
I. Title.
LB1743.S53 1993
371. 1'46—dc20   93-17871
                                                                      CIP

Cover design by Phillip Augusta.
Text design by Merrick Hamilton.
Pre-press production by Kailyard Associates.
Illustrations by Barbara Carter.
Printed on acid-free paper in the United States of America.

93 94 95 96 97   10 9 8 7 6 5 4 3 2

Contents

GO

Acknowledgments

*Professional learning involves standing on the shoulders
of others and joining a community of learners.*

—Lucy Calkins and Shelley Harwayne, 1987

The information included in this handbook was collected from thousands of teachers attending workshops. I asked them to indicate what they liked and didn't like about workshops, and used what they told me to influence the content of the book. I thank them for sharing their insights.

Additionally, I attended the workshops of more than twenty people who earn their living by facilitating workshops for teachers. In subsequent interviews I asked them for specific suggestions as to what made effective workshops for elementary teachers The ideas and strategies they modeled in their workshops and later shared with me in the interviews influenced the content of this handbook, as well. I am especially grateful to the Bureau of Education and Research and the many speakers associated with that organization who gave their time and talent to contribute so much to the content of this book. Specifically, I want to thank the following presenters who kindly shared their expertise with me: Charlene Sutter Arvizu, Michelle Borba, Greg Denman, Jan Donaldson, Marilyn Dow, David Greenberg, Roger Kukes, Lola May, Peggy Richek, Barbara Rothman, Rebecca Sitton, Valerie Welk, and Nancy Whisler. Special thanks to Richard Herzberg, Executive Director of the Bureau of Education and Research, for providing me with the opportunity to talk with and observe so many outstanding presenters.

I researched the topic of effective teacher workshops in countless books and journal articles. Suggestions that seemed appropriate for teachers beginning to facilitate workshops for their peers have been adapted for the handbook. I appreciate those who wrote their good ideas down so that others could learn from them.

The ideas included in this handbook are a combination of my experience as a workshop facilitator and as a workshop participant. Over the years I have learned from many people whose ideas, comments and feedback have greatly influenced the strategies I use in my workshops and the suggestions included in this handbook. If I have inadvertently omitted giving credit to people for their original idea, I apologize.

I also want to acknowledge the experts who agreed to evaluate this manuscript in its initial and final stages. These people have significant experience and knowledge about workshop facilitation, and shared their insights to make this handbook better. Special thanks go to Paul Burden, Gary Ferrington, Kathie Forman, Rich Herzberg, Joellen Killion, Frank Koontz, Judy Olson, Donald Orlich, Nancy Polette, and Dennis Sparks.

Most especially, I want to express my appreciation to my husband John Chamberlain who encouraged and supported me as I commuted cross-country to Columbia University to complete my research that eventually led to this book. It's finally done!

Acknowledgments
───────────
x

ON YOUR MARK

First things first
—Proverb

Before you concentrate on the process of facilitating a workshop for teachers, you should take into account some preliminary information. In this section I present the guiding principles for the handbook as well as some definitions and considerations about effective workshops and workshop facilitators.

★

1

Introduction

Sharing your good ideas through a workshop for your colleagues is one of the best ways you can challenge yourself to grow professionally. Facilitating such a workshop gives you an opportunity to share what you know and to reflect on your teaching as you determine how best to communicate your knowledge. You are to be commended for taking this opportunity to enhance both yourself and your profession.

Teachers Teaching Teachers: A Sound Idea for Professional Development

According to Lucy Calkins and Shelley Harwayne (1987), "There is a fine line between teaching others how to teach and teaching oneself how to teach" (p. 15). Their experiences with teachers training teachers in the Teachers College Writing Project at Columbia University have demonstrated how effectively teachers share and teach their peers in professional development. Bruce Joyce and Beverly Showers (1988) have completed significant research that corroborates this view of teachers teaching and working with their own peers. They encourage the use of teacher-facilitated workshops because

- good teaching is everywhere, and good teachers are potential staff developers
- teachers learn readily from other teachers
- development of better teaching practices should be supported
- they link teachers who are interested in improving their teaching to teachers who have similar interests

P. C. Wu (1987) further identifies six reasons classroom teachers say they favor other teachers as workshop facilitators: teachers as consultants know what is occurring day to day in the classroom; teacher consultants create a comfortable atmosphere, facilitating the exchange of ideas; teacher-directed workshops tend to involve active participation; teacher-led workshops are usually practical and immediately applicable to the classroom; teacher consultants understand the resources and time available to teachers; teacher-led workshops provide more consultants with less expense. And as Linda Lambert (1988) points out, mentor teacher and similar programs support the idea that "teachers must believe they can be the chief architects of their own knowledge and the primary knowledge generators of the profession" (p. 666).

Using This Handbook

There are many manuals and handbooks intended to train the trainer. This handbook is different, however, because it does not present a single formula that a particular workshop faciliator should follow to create the perfect workshop. Instead, this handbook provides a number of ideas that any facilitator can choose from to incorporate into any workshop. Just as people have different learning and teaching styles (Guild and Garger, 1985), they have unique styles of leading workshops. Calkins and Harwayne (1987) suggest that workshop facilitators, like writers, need to find their own voices. What is effective in one workshop for one facilitator may be totally ineffective in another situation or with another facilitator. Rather than trying to emulate someone else's approach, find your own strengths and use them in your workshops. Learn to trust your intuition and instincts, and adapt other people's ideas and suggestions to suit your personal facilitation style. One of the most important characteristics of an effective workshop facilitator is authenticity—plan and conduct your workshops in a way that reflects your personality.

Throughout this handbook you will be urged to reflect upon your personal experiences as a teacher who has attended teacher workshops. Such reflection will make you aware of how a particular workshop facilitator's behavior either motivated or hindered your learning. You will also be asked to draw on your background as a classroom teacher to guide you in becoming an effective workshop facilitator. Several of these reflecting activities are preceded by a pencil symbol to remind you that you may want to jot down your thoughts.

This handbook, then, is not meant to be a prescription but a compilation of suggestions and ideas that have been gleaned through my own experience as a workshop facilitator and from dozens of others who plan and present workshops for teachers. The advice presented here is practical, useful, and effective. Read through this handbook and choose those ideas most likely to work for you. Only you can decide which will best adapt to your particular situation. Making these decisions is the essence of workshop facilitation. Whether you are planning a brief presentation at a professional conference or a longer workshop for other teachers, you can follow certain strategies to increase the likelihood that everyone—the teachers attending the workshop and you, the facilitator—will be satisfied that it has been a worthwhile educational experience.

Workshop Defined

The term *workshop* has come to mean everything from a speech before a group to a strategy-planning session among co-workers. In this handbook *workshop* indicates a group meeting of teachers with the primary purpose of learning. A presentation at a professional conference, a sharing session at a district inservice day, an appearance as a guest lecturer in a college course, or a multihour program in which teachers hear and learn about what works in your classroom are all various forms of workshops under this definition. As I sometimes describe it, in a workshop the facilitator does the *work* of planning how to share ideas so that the participants can *shop* through the suggestions (i.e., learn) in order to identify the ones that will work best for them.

Thomas Sork (1984) offers the following advantages and disadvantages to the workshop instructional format that should be considered in planning a program.

Participants can apply the learning from a workshop relatively quickly. Teachers can use what they learn in the workshop without having to wait for the conclusion of a longer class. This is why teachers have come to expect many ready-to-use ideas in a workshop.

People tend to interact with others in unique and interesting ways because of the intense nature of the workshop. When teachers come together for a limited amount of time to learn as much as possible, they are encouraged to tap all of the resources available, including their colleagues. Their rich and varied backgrounds are excellent learning resources for all participants.

Participants may be away from their usual working environments. A change of scenery can motivate and encourage learning. Teachers away from the everyday distractions and concerns of the classroom can concentrate on the workshop experience itself and gain from its less stressful environment.

Workshops are focused learning environments. Teachers who attend a workshop often have some common experiences and common goals. This shared focus helps everyone work together during the limited time available.

The same workshop is adaptable to various groups' needs. One basic workshop can be changed somewhat for different groups and presented a number of times. The content and strategies for sharing that content can be readily adapted to meet any number of teacher and situational needs.

A variety of instructional and learning strategies can be incorporated into a single workshop. Various techniques can be used to accommodate the different learning styles and preferences of the participants. A workshop is flexible enough to allow for lecture, small group work, reading, writing, discussions, and other approaches in one instructional format.

There is a danger of information overload in a workshop. Workshops are intensive learning experiences, with participants trying to get as much as they can in the short time. This can lead to feeling fatigued or being overwhelmed.

External factors can have a significant impact on the workshop. Equipment failures, overcrowding, and late beginnings have a much greater impact on a workshop than in longer learning situations because there is no extra time to compensate for unexpected delays.

There is a limited amount of time for feedback. Because the teachers are in the workshop for such a brief period, there is little opportunity to provide any type of feedback to the participants either during the workshop or as a follow-up. Some participants may write or contact the facilitator about a question, but most will receive next to no feedback as they implement ideas and suggestions from the workshop.

Those who attend workshops are not always those who are most comfortable in participatory learning activities. Although the workshop format encourages learners to become involved, some who attend may avoid taking an active part. If the workshop facilitator is not particularly adept at encouraging participation, the group process techniques that make the workshop unique may even become obstacles to its success.

Facilitator Defined

In this handbook, *facilitator* refers to the person who is leading the workshop. Sometimes the workshop leaders will be instructing the adult students. At other times workshop leaders are presenters, sharing new information. On still other occasions they are guides, assisting teachers in investigating new ideas. In each of these situations, the overall goal is for the teachers to learn as a result of the experience. Learning is a process, and a process is facilitated. The workshop leader, then, is a facilitator of the participating teachers' learning.

In Conclusion

Planning and facilitating a workshop or presentation for your colleagues is a significant step in your professional growth. When you share your good ideas with other teachers, you have an opportunity not only to expand your personal knowledge but also to share your professional expertise with others. In this chapter we examined the advantages and disadvantages of the workshop format and explored a number of strategies and techniques you can use as a workshop facilitator to encourage the professional growth of peers.

Works Cited and Suggested Readings

Barkley, William B.; McCormick, William J.; and Taylor, Robin R. "Teachers as Workshop Leaders." *Journal of Staff Development,* 8 (Summer 1987): 45–48

Calkins, Lucy M.; and Harwayne, Shelley. *The Writing Workshop: A World of Difference.* Chapter 2. Portsmouth, NH: Heinemann, 1987

Carter, Maggie; and Powell, Debbie. "Teacher Leaders as Staff Developers." *Journal of Staff Development,* 13 (Winter 1992): 8–12

Dillon-Peterson, B. "Reflections on the Development of a Staff Developer." *Journal of Staff Development,* 3 (Summer 1982): 6–11

Galbraith, Michael W. "Essential Skills for the Facilitator of Adult Learning." *Lifelong Learning,* 12 (April 1989): 10–13

Ginocchio, Frederick L. "Teacher-Clinicians Put Credibility into Staff Development." *Journal of Staff Development,* 11 (Spring 1990): 16–18

Guild, Pat B.; and Garger, Stephen. *Marching to Different Drummers.* Alexandria, VA: Association for Supervision and Curriculum Development, 1985

Joyce, Bruce; and Showers, Beverly. *Student Achievement Through Staff Development.* New York: Longman, 1988

Lambert, Linda. "Staff Development Redesigned." *Phi Delta Kappa,* 69 (May 1988): 665–668

Moye, M. Jack; and Rodgers, Kathrine M. "Teachers as Staff Developers: A Success Story." *Journal of Staff Development,* 8 (Spring 1987): 42–44

Neilsen, Lorri. "Of Parachutes, Mockingbirds and Bat-Poets: A New Paradigm for Professional Growth." Part 1. *Reading Teacher,* 45 (September 1991): 64–66

———. "Of Parachutes, Mockingbirds and Bat-Poets: A New Paradigm for Professional Growth." Part 2. *Reading Teacher,* 45 (November 1991): 240–241

Saxl, Ellen; Lieberman, Ann; and Miles, Matthew. "Help Is at Hand: New Knowledge for Teachers as Staff Developers." *Journal of Staff Development,* 8 (Spring 1987): 7–11

Sork, Thomas J. "The Workshop as a Unique Instructional Format." In
Designing and Implementing Effective Workshops, edited by Thomas J.
Sork. San Francisco: Jossey-Bass, 1984

Wu, P. C. "Teachers as Staff Developers: Research, Opinions and Cautions."
Journal of Staff Development, 8 (Spring 1987): 4–6

2

Effective Teacher Workshops

All of us have been to workshops during our teaching careers. Sometimes we leave a session thinking that our time was well spent, that we learned a great deal. We have any number of ideas to mull over and strategies to try out. We feel good about the workshop and would recommend it to other teachers. We have also attended workshops that are not nearly so successful. We feel that we wasted our time, learning little or no thought-provoking or useful information. What makes the difference?

Characteristics of an Effective Workshop Facilitator

What makes someone an effective workshop facilitator? Throughout this book you will read of various strategies people have used during workshops they've facilitated for teachers. These ideas are appropriate for most presentations and many different facilitators. The ideas alone, however, will not turn you into a successful workshop facilitator. Your individual style and presence also play a part in how well you lead workshops.

Many expert facilitators have identified the same three essential characteristics of one who runs effective workshops for teachers. First, you need a thorough understanding of and passion for your workshop subject. Choose a topic in which you have not only research-based knowledge but also extensive experience; teachers need to know that you have put the theory into practice. Your passion will fuel your enthusiasm to learn more about the topic, and teachers will catch that infectious enthusiasm as they take part in the workshop. Your knowledge will give you the confidence you need to make the work-

Think of a person whose workshop you especially appreciated. Make a list of those characteristics of the facilitator that had the greatest impact on your feelings about the workshop. How can you use this list to guide you as a workshop facilitator?

shop look effortless, and your sincerity and commitment to the topic will be evident. Your self-confidence and poise as a speaker depend to a great extent on your ability to relax and be natural. The more familiar you are with a subject, the more relaxed you will be. When you know and care about your subject and your participants, you can concentrate all of your energy on your message and your workshop—so none will be left over for nervousness and insecurity.

The second essential characteristic is flexibility. As a workshop facilitator, you need to be fully prepared for the unexpected. If you assume that almost anything can (and will) go wrong, you are not being a pessimist but rather a pragmatist who is not going to allow some situations beyond your control to wreak havoc with an otherwise smoothly running workshop. Learn to go with the flow and change what you can but leave the rest of the worrying to someone else. This flexibility also extends to the plans you make for your workshop content and activities. If what you're doing isn't working, modify it. You would make the switch in the classroom, and the same thing applies in a workshop for adults. A workshop facilitator needs to be fully prepared but also willing to abandon certain preparations if they are not meeting the participants' needs.

Finally, a workshop facilitator must be genuine. You are what you are, and the workshop participants will appreciate it if you convey that realness. A facade may work for awhile, but eventually people will see through it. Be yourself, and you won't have to work nearly as hard as you would if you pretend to be someone you're not. Let the participants know that you care about them and that you are sincere in your efforts to do everything you can to make the workshop a successful experience for everyone.

Why Me? Your Personal Strengths as a Workshop Facilitator

As a workshop facilitator, you may initially undergo what Stephen Brookfield (1990) identifies as the

You're ready to stretch yourself professionally by conducting a workshop for your colleagues. Each workshop facilitator has particular expertise and talents. Think about the qualities you have that would help you to be an effective workshop facilitator. What positive remarks do you hear from students and their parents about your teaching? Talk with your friends and colleagues for additional ideas. Keep this list close at hand as you begin planning your workshop so you can take advantage of your assets.

impostor syndrome. You may wonder what you could have to share that all those teachers, some with substantially more experience than you, could possibly be interested in learning. All you see is their wealth of experience and ideas, and you may think that what you have to offer pales in comparison. Take comfort in knowing that most workshop facilitators have felt this way at various times in their careers. Do a self-perception check to help you identify your strengths as a workshop facilitator.

> Make a list of what has appealed to you in workshops you've attended. As you're listing these attributes, think about what you especially liked regarding facilitator characteristics, workshop content, workshop activities, media and materials, and physical arrangements.

From the Teachers: What Works in Teacher Workshops

No one knows better than teachers what is effective in teacher workshops. Use your own experience to help you identify what works for you in teacher workshops. For example, you might have attended a workshop where the presenter moved too quickly through the material. Remembering this, you can try to pace your workshop so that the participants have a chance to ask questions and grasp the content.

Hundreds of teachers were asked what made a workshop effective for them; following is a summary of their comments. Use what your colleagues say to help you design and conduct a dynamic workshop.

Facilitator Characteristics

Teachers like facilitators who are

enthusiastic and interested in the topic
dynamic and able to stimulate excitement
open, honest, and friendly
patient when answering questions
respectful of the participants
humorous and warm
knowledgeable about the topic
well organized
able to stay on the topic
experienced as a teacher
willing to share personal stories and experiences
mindful of details

Workshop Content

Teachers have very specific ideas about what is effective regarding workshop content. Many of their comments are procedural in that they like to have

clear objectives

a schedule that is followed

procedures explained

clear directions for activities

lots of examples

concrete ideas that are immediately useful

attention-grabbing content

research and theory to support applications

In addition the content needs to be

well organized

based upon preassessed participant needs

Workshop Activities

Teachers have strong opinions about the activities in a workshop. They like

active involvement

a balance between group participation and presentation of information

demonstrations of ideas and strategies with classroom examples

demonstrations of materials and ideas that have immediate use in the
classroom

lots of interaction

a variety of activities

an appropriate amount of sharing among participants

Media and Materials

Teachers indicate that media and materials are important. There should be some variety in the visuals, and all materials need to be up-to-date. Teachers like to receive either a booklet of accompanying materials for the workshop or a handout to go with and extend the workshop.

Physical Arrangements

The physical comfort of the teachers matters, as well. Items they specifically mention are

appropriate seating arrangements for group size and type of activity

comfortable room temperature

good acoustics

easy-to-see visuals and facilitator

appropriate breaks

availability of food and water

adult-sized tables

sessions at times other than right after school

Compare the teachers' comments about workshops with what you have observed. This combined information can provide the foundation for planning and implementing a workshop for your colleagues.

In Conclusion

In this chapter we explored the three key qualities that make a good facilitator—extensive knowledge of and a passion for the workshop topic, flexibility, and sincerity. We also looked at teachers' ideas about the characteristics of an effective workshop. Most important is that you remember to use what *you* know about workshops as you begin to plan how to share your good ideas with other teachers in a workshop format.

Works Cited and Suggested Readings

Brookfield, Stephen. *The Skillful Teacher*. Chapter 4. San Francisco: Jossey-Bass, 1990

———. *Understanding and Facilitating Adult Learning*. Chapter 6.
San Francisco: Jossey-Bass, 1986

Draves, William A. *How to Teach Adults*. Chapter 3. Manhattan, KS:
Learning Resources Network, 1984

Knox, A. B. *Helping Adults Learn*. Chapter 3. San Francisco: Jossey-Bass, 1987

Spring, Ellen R., et al. "The Best-Ever Workshop." *Book Report,* 4
(January/February 1986): 16–19

3

Guiding Principles

The suggestions and ideas I present in this handbook are shaped by experience and research. Before I go on to specific strategies for running workshops for teachers, I'd like to identify and describe the central principles that influenced the development and selection of materials for this book.

Because Your Students Are Adults

Only within recent years have people considered the unique characteristics of adults as learners. Although teaching adults is similar to teaching children, certain features about adults and how they learn mean that you need to plan and facilitate workshops differently when the participants are adults rather than children. Consider which strategies you know have been successful when teaching children. Then think how you might adapt those strategies when facilitating workshops for teachers.

Your experience as a classroom teacher will certainly be useful when you teach adults, but you should take into account some additional factors.

Make a list of the characteristics of lessons you plan for your students. Review your list and star those ideas that are absolutely essential. Now look at your list again and circle those must-do items you would include in a workshop for teachers. Use these symbols to think about the similarities and differences between learners who are adults and those who are children.

How Adults Learn from Personal Experience

As you think about how adults learn, use your most important resource—yourself. Recall how you learned significant things in your life. Donald Graves's (1989) personal learning history approach, introduced in his book *Discover Your Own Literacy,* may help you remember details about a personal learning experience. He suggests that you identify the significant lesson, the other person or people involved, and any particular memories or experiences associated with this learning. After you've identified the major components of the learning incident, write out the specifics of the situation; then analyze the learning sequence: Why did you want to learn the new skill or information? What worked? What were the problems? Use this analysis to help you determine some of what you'll need to consider as you plan learning experiences for teachers in your workshop.

Here, for example, are the components that went into my learning to use a computer:

Significant Learning	Other Person Involved	Notes
Operate computer	Daughter	Faster
		Manual

As I began facilitating more and more workshops, it was difficult for me to organize the instructional materials I was producing as well as keep track of correspondence and of my business account. I was talking with my daughter about the problem one day. She suggested that I get a computer, as that would be the most logical way to organize and would help me do what I needed to do more quickly. At her college she was using a particular brand of computer, and she wanted one to use at home, so it seemed reasonable for me to learn to use the same computer. After we purchased the computer, my daughter and I sat down, and she showed me the basics—how to turn it on, particular keys that were important to know, and so on. She watched me do these things, helped me if I needed it, then suggested that I play the cassette tape that came as a guide to the machine and follow the steps on the computer tutorial program. Once she had made sure I got started all right, she left me to practice on my own. The more I practiced, the more proficient I became on the computer, and the more comfortable I was experimenting with new things. Of course, my daughter was available if I had any questions or problems. After the initial work on the computer, I began referring to the manual to answer questions I had.

An analysis of my learning to use the computer suggests the following: First, there was a *need* for the learning. My business was expanding, and I had to have a way to manage the paperwork. Second, there was *motivation* for the learning. It was going to help me to do my job more quickly and efficiently. Third, I had a *model* to show me the task. My daughter sat with me at the computer and demonstrated the basic procedures. Next, the teacher provided *feedback.* My daughter watched while I did what she demonstrated and helped me when necessary; she was also there later to answer further questions. Then I focused on *practice.* I sat at the computer and went through the basic tasks. Throughout the process I used *various presentation formats.* I listened to a cassette tape and followed a tutorial program, then turned to the manual for additional information. An important part of the learning was *discovery.* As I became familiar with the computer, I experimented more.

As you analyze your learning sequence, you'll find that some of the steps necessary for adult learning are obvious.

Characteristics of Adult Learners

In planning your workshop, be aware of the following factors that specifically affect adult learning.

Adults have many experiences that are relevant to and affect their learning. Adults bring all life experiences, both past and present, personal and professional, to bear on what they learn (Brookfield, 1986). Workshop strategies need to complement and incorporate this knowledge and experience. When planning workshops for teachers, design activities that acknowledge and apply such expertise, giving the adults an opportunity to reflect on and process the information and activities of the workshop in light of their backgrounds.

Adults' experiences are a rich resource for one another. The variety of life experiences adults carry into a workshop is an invaluable asset. Teachers can learn much from a dialog with their peers; allow time for teachers to share their related experiences with others.

The understanding of new knowledge is influenced by previous knowledge. Prior learning is integral to and affects adults' new learning (Brookfield, 1986). Build upon that prior learning in teachers' workshops by acknowledging the teachers' familiarity with a concept as you introduce more information about the concept.

Many adults are problem-solving learners and often seek out learning because they have a use for the knowledge (Kidd, 1993). Transfer of new ideas to current situations is important for many adults. When J. W. C. Johnstone and R. Rivera (1965) first investigated reasons for adults to participate in learning activities, they concluded that "the major emphasis in adult learning is on the practical rather than the academic; on the applied rather than the theoretical; and on skills rather than on knowledge or information" (p. 3). K. Patricia Cross (1981) indicates that nothing in the many surveys of adult learners significantly changes this conclusion. Therefore, as you plan your workshop, highlight ways that teachers will be able to integrate the content of the workshop into their classrooms and other teaching situations.

Adults have many concerns outside of the workshop situation that may affect their learning. What adults want to learn and the ways in which they learn are often determined by external factors (Merriam and Caffarella, 1991). Learning seldom occurs "in splendid isolation from the world in which the learner lives; . . . it is intimately related to that world and affected by it" (Jarvis, 1987, p. 11). Obstacles to learning emanate from family, personal, and community responsibilities, as well as from social pressures on the job. As you're planning and conducting your workshop, be aware of personal and professional contextual factors that may affect the teachers' ability to respond. Teachers ready to go on strike, for example, may not be thinking about how to teach their students to read.

Adults can be self-directed, self-motivated managers of their personal learning. Continued learning depends upon achieving satisfaction, which learners often identify as making progress toward their own learning goals (Brookfield, 1986). The content of the workshop needs to be organized and presented according to the predicted needs and interests of the teachers, so that ultimately they can go beyond what is presented in the workshop to plan their own study.

Adults learn in a variety of ways, and there is not just one correct method of learning (Knox, 1987). Adults' learning styles influence how they learn: some prefer to read for information, some prefer to listen, others like to discuss, and others enjoy writing (Claxton and Ralston, 1987). Consider that the teachers in the workshop like to learn in different ways and provide various learning opportunities to accommodate these styles.

Certain age-related characteristics have an impact on adult learning (Bee, 1987). Age may affect the length of time it takes an adult to learn (Cross, 1981). While middle-aged and older adults can easily learn, it may take them somewhat longer to grasp new concepts than it does their younger colleagues. Some of the older teachers may need more time to practice a new skill and more examples of a new strategy. Recognize that teachers of various ages will be attending the workshop, and provide activities and strategies appropriate for all. Also keep in mind that older adults may need more light, more volume, and may have other special physical needs.

Principles for Effective Teacher Workshops

Fifteen years of facilitating workshops and extensive research into the field have helped me to identify certain underlying principles for workshop facilitation. Each of the ideas, suggestions, activities, and strategies I present in this handbook are based on these principles.

The participants' experiences are important in the learning situation and need to be incorporated into the workshop. As we have seen, adults bring extensive experience to the workshop. Honor that experience by allowing the participants to incorporate it as part of the learning process (Pike, 1989). Effective workshops tap participants' experiences as a major resource for their learning and provide opportunities for participants to share related experiences with others (Brookfield, 1986; Knowles, 1980).

While there are similarities between teaching children and adults, specific adult-oriented presentation, communication, and facilitation skills must be incorporated into workshops for teachers. The facilitator needs to be aware of adult needs for learning and accommodate those in workshop facilitation style and strategies (Seaman and Fellenz, 1989). Participants should always be treated as adults and involved in activities that are appropriate to their adult status; asking adults to "pretend" they are the age of their students can be offensive. Many adults will appreciate acknowledgment of their skills and experiences and may expect to use these during the workshop as they share and interact with others. Short lecture presentations effectively delivered are usually best suited for adult audiences.

Participants need to be actively involved in their own learning, and any workshop or presentation requires such involvement. Activities, strategies, and suggestions throughout this book are intended to allow participants opportunities to listen, to talk, to view, to write, to read, and, above all, to think. Participatory learning methods help ensure that knowledge, concepts, and skills are understandable in terms of the adults' own experiences (Brookfield, 1986). Without involvement there is little reason for the audience to care. People learn more when they are actively involved in the learning process than when they are passively involved (Pike, 1989).

Participation strategies need to be natural and meaningful to adult learners. Adults like to be in charge and dislike being manipulated into doing things that seem silly and meaningless (Seaman and Fellenz, 1989). Activities that seem irrelevant to the workshop topic and the teachers' needs may be perceived as a waste of time and as childish. Teachers must have the option of participating and should feel no negative consequences for a decision not to participate in a particular activity.

Because learners learn in different ways, different instructional strategies should be used in a workshop. Adults prefer to learn in different ways, so it is necessary to incorporate a variety of techniques in order to accommodate each of the preferences (Merriam, 1989). Some participants will want to listen to an idea, others to try it out; some will want to discuss it, others to discover it for themselves (Guild and Garger, 1985). Discussions, presentation of information, role-plays, and case study analysis are just a few of the techniques that can be effectively employed in workshops. It is important to involve as many senses as possible to help participants understand and know how to apply the information shared. Be ready to explain ideas in at least three different ways or using three different types of examples. Diversity is crucial to every workshop.

Visuals such as overhead transparencies, videos, still pictures, charts, and graphs can enhance the workshop presentation. Many people find that visuals help them to better understand a concept. Because people are accustomed to visual stimulation, workshop facilitators need to remember to include visuals as they plan their workshop.

Once it has been presented, new material should be modeled through practice in the workshop. Participants who have an opportunity to practice new ideas and concepts with others and under supervision before trying them independently become more confident (Loucks-Horsley, 1987). Supervised practice during a workshop can provide the feedback that is conducive to continued learning.

Participants are interested in knowing how they can apply the content of the workshop. Central to the adult learner's curriculum are situations or problems the learner faces (Yakowicz, 1989). It is therefore important to help teachers identify the applications of the workshop strategies and content to their personal teaching situations.

Any workshop, no matter how short, needs to be prepared. Facilitators must be thoroughly ready and organized for a presentation. If the workshop is not well prepared, the participants may concentrate on the lack of organization rather than on the content of the presentation. Further, it is both insulting and embarrassing to the participants when the facilitator has not taken the time necessary to prepare adequately.

A climate of respect is important in workshops. How the adults are treated in the learning situation will affect their total learning experience. Participants should be valued as unique individuals deserving of respect from the facilitator and other participants alike (Brookfield, 1986). If teachers are treated with respect, they will infer that they are highly regarded individuals, and some positive incidental learning will have occurred. Although the teachers are not specifically aware of that learning, their future reactions may be changed because of the experience.

Workshop facilitators need to be enthusiastic about what they are presenting. Enthusiasm is an effective inspiration for incidental learning. Adults are aware of the enthusiasm presenters have for topics and may share that enthusiasm as well. Genuine excitement is contagious, and participants who catch it may then transfer it to the topic of the workshop.

Facilitators should present workshops on topics in which they are knowledgeable. Knowledgeable workshop facilitators are usually confident in their roles. Because the content of the workshops is determined by the participants' needs, facilitators need to be prepared for unplanned questions and occurrences. Only when facilitators have an extra reservoir of knowledge on a topic can they feel ready for the unexpected.

Participants expect that the facilitator will have experiential knowledge as well as intellectual knowledge. Participants often want to know that what is shared in a workshop is based on both theoretical and personal experience. Citing practical experience validates what is said and adds credibility to the workshop. Illustrations and examples need to be balanced between triumphs and mistakes; participants can become discouraged if they think the facilitator only succeeds.

The role of a workshop leader is to facilitate learning, not to impose learning. The workshop leader is there to guide the teachers in their learning, but the leader cannot force them to learn. Provide numerous ideas and strategies with the notion that teachers will learn from and choose those that seem most appropriate for them.

There needs to be a balance between information and interaction in workshops. Teachers want to hear worthwhile insights; provide a research base for the information you share. Be sure, too, that the teachers have ample opportunity to process this information; give them time to think about, talk about, and experiment with the information.

In Conclusion

Stephen Brookfield (1990) suggests that all teachers—teachers who facilitate workshops as well as classroom teachers—develop a personal vision of teaching to guide instructional decisions. This rationale should include the values and convictions that inform the decisions and set the aims and purposes for instruction. The principles outlined in this chapter are the basis of my vision of effective workshop facilitation. Consider them as you develop your own reasons for the decisions you make in planning and conducting workshops for teachers.

Works Cited and Suggested Readings

Bee, Helen L. *The Journey of Adulthood.* Chapters 1, 2, and 5. New York: Macmillan, 1987

Brookfield, Stephen. *Understanding and Facilitating Adult Learning.*
San Francisco: Jossey-Bass, 1986

——————. *The Skillful Teacher.* San Francisco: Jossey-Bass, 1990

Claxton, C. S.; and Ralston, Y. *Learning Styles: Implications for Improving
Educational Practices.* Washington, D.C.: ERIC Clearinghouse on Higher
Education, 1987

Conti, Gary J.; and Welborn, Ruth B. "Teaching-Learning Styles and the Adult
Learner." *Lifelong Learning,* 9 (June 1986): 20–24

Cross, K. Patricia. *Adults as Learners.* San Francisco: Jossey- Bass, 1981

Dalellew, Tesfatsion; and Martinez, Yvonne. "Andragogy and Development: A
Search for the Meaning of Staff Development." *Journal of Staff
Development,* 9 (Summer 1988): 28–31

Even, Mary Jane. "Why Adults Learn in Different Ways." *Lifelong Learning,*
10 (June 1987): 23–26

Graves, Donald H. *Discover Your Own Literacy.* Chapter 6. Portsmouth, NH:
Heinemann, 1989

Gregorc, Anthony. *An Adult's Guide to Style.* Maynard, MA: Gabriel Systems,
1982

Guild, Pat B.; and Garger, Stephen. *Marching to Different Drummers.*
Alexandria, VA: Association for Supervision and Curriculum Development,
1985

Jarvis, P. *Adult Learning in the Social Context.* London: Croom Helm, 1987

Johnstone, J. W. C.; and Rivera, R. *Volunteers for Learning.* Chicago: Aldine,
1965

Kahler, Alan A., et al. *Methods in Adult Education.* Danville, IL: Interstate,
1985

Kidd, J. *How Adults Learn.* New York: Cambridge, 1973

Knowles, Malcolm S. *The Modern Practice of Adult Education: From
Pedagogy to Andragogy.* 2d ed. New York: Cambridge Books, 1980

Knox, Alan B. *Helping Adults Learn.* San Francisco: Jossey-Bass, 1987.

Loucks-Horsley, Susan, et al. *Continuing to Learn: A Guidebook for Teacher
Development.* Oxford, OH: National Staff Development Council, 1987

Merriam, Sharan B., ed. *Being Responsive to Adult Learners.* Glenview, IL:
Scott, Foresman, 1989

Merriam, Sharan B.; and Caffarella, R. S. *Learning in Adulthood.*
San Francisco: Jossey-Bass, 1991

Moore, Janet R. "Guidelines Concerning Adult Learning." *Journal of Staff
Development,* 9 (Summer 1988): 2–5

Pike, Robert W. *Creative Training Techniques Handbook.* Chapter 2. Minneapolis, MN: Lakewood Books, 1989

Rogers, Alan. *Teaching Adults.* Philadelphia: Open University Press, 1986.

Seaman, Don F.; and Fellenz, Robert A. *Effective Strategies for Teaching Adults.* Columbus, OH: Merrill, 1989

Yakowicz, William. "Using What We Know to Develop, Implement, and Administer ABE." New York: Department of Higher and Adult Education, Teachers College, Columbia University, 1989

READY

It takes three weeks to prepare a good ad-lib speech.
—Mark Twain

Preparation and planning are the keys to any good workshop. Success depends on thoughtful and thorough planning. In this section there are suggestions for planning your workshop, from the beginning through to the closing, and important considerations for what comes between.

★ ★

4

Before You Begin

There are certain things to consider before you start to plan the content, presentation strategies, and other workshop elements. By thinking about these in advance, you can make your workshop a unique experience for the participants.

Identify the Topic

As we have seen, workshop facilitators need to be both knowledgeable and passionate about their topic. In other words, you should choose a topic in which you have extensive experience and an understanding of the research that supports your experience, and your knowledge must in turn be supported and fueled by your enthusiasm.

To help you identify an appropriate focus for your workshop, pick a subject that interests to you. Take one minute to write all the key words connected to that subject that could be topics for your workshop. Then evaluate your key words and circle those that are legitimate topics. Star those topics about which you have a special interest. Put a line through those about which you have little or no knowledge. Count the number of topics that are circled, starred, and do not have a line through them—these are the topics most appropriate for you to consider for a workshop at this time. If you have five or more topics in this subject, you are ready to begin planning an extensive workshop around your identified subject. If you have fewer than five topics, either plan a shorter workshop or presentation on the subject or spend some time gathering additional information about those topics you have starred but have crossed out. Be certain that you care enough about the topic to gather the information needed to make that topic the focus for your workshop. You must have a clear understanding of the content in order to share that information with others.

Analyze the Participants

It is helpful to know certain facts about the teachers who will attend your workshop so that you can better meet their educational needs. In your classroom the intellectual and personal needs of your students influence the types of educational experiences you provide. Basing your workshop instructional decisions upon the needs of the teachers attending is also important in determining the best and most appropriate workshop for them.

Participants' Profiles

It is valuable to know who the workshop participants are as well as their backgrounds and expertise in order to help you recognize some common ground and provide opportunities to build rapport. If it isn't possible to learn specific information in advance, make some assumptions based upon the location of the workshop and who has organized it. Use the presumed common background to establish quick rapport between the teachers attending the workshop and between the participants and yourself.

Participants' Concerns

Learn as much as possible about what the participants really care about. Find out about what is happening in the school and school district where the teachers work, the latest concerns and issues in the subject area of the workshop, and so on. By doing so, you won't waste your time (and theirs) talking about something about which they have no concern.

Think about what you know about your students prior to meeting them on the first day of school. List that information: their names, grade levels, and so forth. What does this information lead you to infer about the students? For example, if your students are sophomores in high school, do you make any assumptions about them? List these types of assumptions. Finally, list what you consciously try to find out about your students within the first weeks of school: abilities in specific subject areas, social skills, and any pertinent information about their lives away from school. Add to this list any other data that would help you meet your students' educational needs. Identify which of these facts it would be helpful to know about the teachers who will be part of your workshop. Consider how you can gather this information.

Participants' Knowledge About the Content

Ascertaining how much knowledge the participants have about the topic can let you know how much immediate participation to expect or whether the teachers will need some background knowledge before they feel ready to participate. Awareness of any prior knowledge can also help you plan workshop content and strategies at the appropriate instructional level. You may be able to predict this information from the content of your workshop—an introductory workshop should attract beginners and an advanced workshop should attract teachers with more extensive knowledge. However, be prepared for unexpected situations, as people do not always select workshops appropriate for their level of expertise.

Participants' Experience with Other Workshops on the Topic

Knowing whether the participants have attended other workshops similar to yours and how much background the participants have in your topic will allow you to plan a program that is stimulating but not too advanced. If your workshop is on a topic that many people are familiar with, identify a new twist for yours to make it different from others.

Number of Participants Attending the Workshop

The number of people attending a workshop affects your decisions about the format and types of activities to include. Be forewarned, however, that people make decisions at the last minute, and numbers change up to the beginning of the workshop.

Mandatory or Voluntary Attendance

Whether participants want to or have to attend the workshop often sets the initial tone. If you know in advance that some teachers are simply fulfilling a requirement by attending, you may need to do additional work to convince them of the benefits of having attended.

Gather the Data

When you know the focus of your workshop and you have some sense of who will be attending, you can begin to gather the data that will become the content of the workshop. Gather as much information as possible from a variety of sources. When I am considering a workshop topic, I make a list of books to read, journals that may have pertinent articles, people to talk to, and conferences and workshops to attend; this gives me an outline to use while I am gathering information as well as a record of the sources where I located specific data. Collect insights, anecdotes, and specific tips to incorporate into the workshop as support for the main idea.

Keep a file of materials related to the topic of the workshop, and use those that seem especially relevant to the particular group of participants. If you have an overabundance of material, you can be selective and set high standards for what you include.

Identify the Critical Attribute

Because teachers have the option of attending a variety of workshops, many of which are on the same subject as yours, you need to discover the characteristic or focus that makes your workshop unique.

Identify Workshop Goals and Aims

It is important that you know the central idea and overarching goals for the workshop. Ask yourself the purpose for the workshop, and be certain that you develop content and activities that reflect that aim. As you're pinpointing the workshop purpose, consider why you are facilitating the workshop, what you hope to accomplish during the workshop, and what participants should be able to achieve as a result of attending the workshop.

To help you find what sets your workshop apart from all the others, consider the workshops you have attended on the same subject as yours. For each workshop, identify what made it unique in its subject area. After listing these features, star the workshops that were especially effective. Is there any relationship between the unique characteristic of the workshop and its effectiveness? Next, decide what twist to give your treatment of the topic. If you have not attended many workshops on your topic, interview other teachers who have attended appropriate subject-area workshops.

Facilitator Goals

Determine what you want to have happen in the workshop, and why it is important that it happen. If you have a clear sense of the purpose of the workshop, it will be easier for you to guide off-the-topic questions and discussions back to the workshop purpose. After you have decided these basic goals and aims for the workshop, then you can identify specific strategies and activities that reflect and lead to those goals. I usually keep my goals to fewer than six,

Match your goals as the workshop facilitator with the expected goals of the participants by sharing the description of your workshop with several colleagues. Ask them to list two to five things they think they would learn from the workshop. Compare their goals with the facilitator goals you identified. If there is some discrepancy between the two sets of goals, rewrite the workshop description to reflect more accurately the type of learning you want participants to expect.

focusing on three for an all-day workshop; fewer goals may be appropriate for shorter workshops.

You will also want to know whether your anticipated outcomes or goals for the workshop have been attained. Identify specifically how you will be able to recognize such success.

Goals for Participants

Although you may not be able to talk with the participants individually or personally in advance, at least try to assume from the workshop content what the participants will want to be able to do after having attended your workshop. Goals for participants also include what you want the participants to learn as a result of their taking part in the workshop. Ask the workshop organizer for additional details about the participants, or make some assumptions based upon the publicity for the workshop you're facilitating.

Consider the Logistics

Those details over which you may have little or no control can have a major impact on the workshop if you are not aware of them in advance. However, with some prior knowledge about the workshop location and its facilities and other logistics, you can plan a workshop that is adaptable to these potentially adverse factors—and you may even be able to use them to the benefit of the workshop and its participants.

Time of Day and Length of Workshop

Many people are freshest first thing in the morning and more likely to fade just after lunch. Plan your activities to reflect the time of day during which the workshop is scheduled, energizing participants with more involvement and movement activities in the afternoon, for example. A workshop that occurs directly after school is especially challenging, so be prepared with alternative content and a variety of activities. Confirm the length of the workshop in order to plan an appropriate amount of content and a realistic number of activities.

Workshop Location

Consider the facilities when you plan. If the chairs cannot be moved, then you obviously wouldn't include a number of activities for which people would have to gather into a circle. If the workshop is in a small area, you wouldn't plan activities that require a lot of movement. The only time the facilities are a major problem is when you don't know about them beforehand.

In Conclusion

In this chapter we've looked at some of the factors contributing to the likelihood of success for a workshop that you need to consider before you begin to design specific content and presentation strategies. You should identify the topic, analyze the participants' needs and prior knowledge, gather the data, identify the niche for the workshop, determine workshop goals and aims, and consider logistics such as physical facilities. After you address these preliminary factors, you will be ready to go on to the details of the program.

Works Cited and Suggested Readings

Boyle, Patrick G. *Planning Better Programs.* New York: McGraw-Hill, 1981

Brookfield, Stephen. *Understanding and Facilitating Adult Learning.* Chapters 9 and 10. San Francisco: Jossey-Bass, 1986

Draves, William A. *How to Teach Adults.* Manhattan, KS: Learning Resources Network, 1984

Galbraith, Michael W. "Essential Skills for the Facilitator of Adult Learning." *Lifelong Learning,* 12 (April 1989): 10–13

Knowles, Malcolm S. *The Modern Practice of Adult Education: From Pedagogy to Andragogy.* 2d ed. Chapters 6 and 7. New York: Cambridge, 1980

Knox, Alan B. *Helping Adults Learn.* Chapter 4. San Francisco: Jossey-Bass, 1987

Mills, Sheryl. "Planning a Workshop?" *Developer* (December 1990/January 1991): 1, 7

Pike, Robert W. *Creative Training Techniques Handbook.* Chapter 2. Minneapolis, MN: Lakewood Books, 1989

Smith, Terry C. *Making Successful Presentations: A Self-Teaching Guide.* 2d ed. Chapter 2. New York: John Wiley & Sons, 1991

5

Grab 'Em and Make 'Em Believe: Beginning and Ending the Workshop

Most workshop facilitators agree that a good workshop needs a strong opening and a strong closing: the beginning sets the tone for the workshop, and the ending seals the participants' impressions about the workshop. Many facilitators therefore suggest that you plan the beginning and ending first, and then fill in the workshop sandwich with the content filling.

The Importance of Openings and Closings

Through a motivating start, you set the tone for the workshop, as most participants establish their feelings about the session. The close of the workshop solidifies these feelings and shapes what the participants will do as a result of their attendance.

To prove to yourself how important the beginning and the ending of a presentation are, try this test adapted from a similar one used by Robert Pike (1989). Look at and read aloud the following series of numbers:

3   23   84   11   4   9   14   8   6

Cover the list of numbers and answer the following questions:

What was the first number?
What was the last number?
What was the middle number?

Most people remember the first and final numbers but have more difficulty remembering those in the middle. That people best remember what happens first and what happens last shows just how essential it is to plan the workshop so that the beginning and ending are memorable and directly relate to and reinforce the activities and content that come in between.

The purpose of the introduction is to explain the topic of the workshop, provide its structure, and establish the association that participants have with the content to be presented. The introduction sets the tone for the session, as participants make value-laden decisions about the workshop in the first few minutes. It is extremely important to start off right.

Show energy, enthusiasm, animation, and your personal connection with the workshop. Begin with all the energy you can muster. First impressions count, so project your interest and enthusiasm so that the participants can feel it, too. Start out upbeat and stay that way.

Make eye contact. Move around as you begin and consciously make eye contact with as many people as possible. Let the participants know that you care about them, not the room around you.

Be open and forthcoming. The participants want to know about you as a person. Early in the workshop, share information about yourself and your family so that participants can make a personal as well as professional connection.

Be aware of your appearance. Participants' first impressions are based upon how you look; dress so that you are perceived the way you want teachers to think of you; casual dress indicates a more casual attitude than formal attire, for example. Most importantly, dress in a way that makes you feel comfortable.

Try to get a response from the participants immediately. Having participants do or say something near the beginning of the workshop establishes the perception that they will be actively involved during the session. Develop a task that requires that they talk to each other in the first part of the workshop.

Opening Strategies

Strategies for workshop introductions are intended to focus the participants' attention and to establish a rapport both between the facilitator and the participants and among the participants. It is important that the introduction strategy relate to the content so participants do not become confused; make this connection clear. Because many teachers appreciate ideas they can use in their classrooms right away, extend these introductory ideas into "take-away" ideas by providing the classroom link and instructions for adapting the idea for use with students. Most of the opening strategies that follow are very low risk so that participants will succeed in the workshop from the outset.

Stimulating Questions

Ask questions to stimulate thinking on the topic of your presentation. This helps participants to begin to focus on the topic. You might ask participants what they consider to be the best part of their jobs or what makes them most nervous about the first day of school. As participants share their responses to these questions, they will learn more about other participants' experiences that relate to the workshop topic.

Problem-Posing Questions

You can help participants begin to think about the topic of the workshop by posing questions that require the teachers to identify problems and possible solutions. For example, a problem-posing question could be What trouble do instructors have when they want to change their method of teaching math? Teachers may identify problems such as parents who don't understand the new technique, lack of materials, and so on. A solution-generating question could be What happens when we communicate with parents about a new method for teaching math? These questions can become the focus outline of the workshop. To emphasize the connection, you might say something to the effect that, "You've posed an interesting and important problem. After the workshop, you will have some answers to the questions that arise when you change your method of teaching math."

Personal Anecdote Story

Share a personal experience or anecdote to which the participants can relate and that is linked to the topic of the workshop. Here would be one such story:

My first year teaching I had a student I'll never forget. I'll call her Leslie. She has gotten funnier as the years passed, but she certainly wasn't funny when she was in my classroom.

I'll never forget one particular school assembly. You know what they're like—the students are sitting on the floor in rows, and the teachers are sitting in folding chairs at the end of the rows. If you watch, before long you'll see a teacher snap her fingers and point to a student. Then you see the student walking down the row to take the space next to the teacher. The assembly had just started when I "snapped" at Leslie. She hadn't been sitting next to me very long when I decided I needed to stand up and lean against the wall. Leslie couldn't resist and began playing with the folded chair. She was more surprised than I when she got her head stuck between the seat and the back of the chair. We had to dismantle the chair to get her head out.

Imagine my surprise and delight when I read that I'm not the only teacher who has had this experience—it happened to Johanna Hurwitz when she taught, and she relates the episode in her book Class Clown.

Sharing this story tells the participants that I am one of them and can make the connections among the workshop topic, facilitator, and participants.

Critical Incidents

Teachers might also be encouraged to describe a professional experience related to the topic of the workshop that has a particular significance for them. A facilitator of a reading workshop might begin the session by asking participants to recall books they enjoyed as children: "Think about a book you read as a child that you really liked—one that made you say 'I'm going to remember this one!' What is the title of the book? Who were the characters? When did you read it? What made the book so memorable?" When participants discuss their favorite books, they learn about one another's reading interests as well as the significance of reading in their lives. If the importance of reading is to be discussed during the workshop, these reminiscences are a natural way to introduce the concept.

Critical incidents may also assess participants' needs relating to the topic: teachers may describe a professional experience linked to the topic of the workshop that has special meaning for them. During a workshop on teacher-related stress, for instance, participants might be asked, "At what point in your teaching career did you say to yourself, 'Perhaps teaching isn't really the career for me'? What was the particular situation or event that caused you to think this? When did it occur? What made it so frustrating?"

The resulting descriptions would indicate the actual experiences, needs, and concerns of the participants that can be incorporated as the workshop progresses. Stephen Brookfield (1990) reminds us that the critical incident technique is successful only if workshop participants have some previous knowledge of or experience with the topic of the workshop.

Sentence Completions

Begin a sentence that relates to the topic of the workshop and ask participants to complete it. Two of my favorites are "I know it's a good book when . . ." and "A teacher is like an eggbeater when . . . ." As teachers share how they completed these sentence fragments, they learn about one another's perceptions of the workshop topic. These are excellent discussion starters, as most of the sentence completions need additional explanation for clearer understanding.

Humorous Stories Based on Real-Life Experiences

Tell a funny story that participants can appreciate. A story based upon a school experience is effective because most teachers have had a similar experience, have heard about one like it, or are glad the situation hasn't happened to them. Shared-experience stories are great for developing camaraderie.

I often tell one story I originally heard in a workshop. It is about an overly enthusiastic teacher.

It was a beautiful spring day, and a gorgeous blue jay landed outside the classroom window in the school yard. The teacher used the students' interest in the bird as motivation for her theme about blue jays. She went to the library and got all the materials she could find about blue jays. The students read about blue jays, they wrote research reports about blue jays, they made up stories about blue jays, they drew pictures of blue jays, they made up math problems about blue jays; they did everything possible that had to do with blue jays.

One day, the blue jay flew into the closed window, hit the glass, and died.

"Good!" said one student who spoke for many. "The blue jay's dead! Now we don't have to study it anymore."

Everybody has become overly zealous about a good idea. This story uses humor to remind teachers that it is possible to kill a good idea by doing too much.

Eye-Catching Visuals

Projecting an image that is humorous, imaginative, or otherwise provocative can focus the participants' attention on the topic. Comic strips, editorial pages, and children's books are good sources. Remember to check the copyright laws and secure any permission necessary before using the materials.

A transparency that always gets teachers' attention shows two young students: one is a boy with pencil in hand, ready to write; the other is a girl whose expression clearly shows her less-than-enthusiastic feeling about writing. The look on her face is one that all teachers have seen on students when they are not excited about schoolwork, and it always generates laughter. Participants' response to these visuals acknowledges the connection between their own experiences and the workshop topic. Sometimes you will want to discuss their reaction; at other times you will need to allow them time to reflect upon it.

Provocative Statements and Statistics

Surprise the participants with an unexpected and unusual statement relating to the topic of the workshop—for example, "There is only one way to teach reading." An unexpected remark is even more effective if you can involve the participants so that they come up with the statistics:

> *The International Reading Association recently completed a study regarding what motivates students to read. Think about your students and predict how many of them like to complete book reports. It is not surprising to learn that only 3 percent of the students surveyed indicated that book reports were a factor that motivated them to read more books.*

When using statistics, be certain that you have the documentation to prove what you say.

Promises

At the beginning of the workshop, tell the participants what they will learn as a result of the session. Make sure the promise is both true and attention-getting. You might say, "By the end of this workshop you will have at least six ideas you can use with your students tomorrow" or "By the end of this workshop you will have at least ten methods that will motivate your students to read but that do not require any special materials or any extra preparation time." At the conclusion of the workshop, remind or ask the participants how the promise was fulfilled.

Unique Demonstrations

Do something intriguing that will gain the participants' attention. I often use props to tell a story. One of my favorites is about a dog named Mack who has a particular appetite for cake. The story is based on the cumulative tale "The House That Jack Built." In Rose Robart's *The Cake That Mack Ate,* the ingredients are revealed one at a time from inside the cake. As each new ingredient is named, all previously mentioned ingredients are also identified.

Some workshop facilitators do magic tricks, share props, or do a dramatic sequence. Once again, be certain that your demonstration relates to the topic at hand.

You Can Bet on It

An effective way to assess participants' knowledge about a topic and to get people to begin socializing with one another is by using a true-false quiz with betting as an extra incentive. Present five to ten statements—some true and some false—that reflect the research on the topic of the workshop. Working individually, the participants indicate which statements they believe to be true and which false. Then they pair off to compare their answers, identify a statement on which they disagree, and try to convince one another of the right answer.

Because people generally want to know the correct answers, share the results of the research. Before they hear the results, however, the teachers need to put their money where their mouths are. They're each "given" $100 as betting money, and they place bets on their first answer, using whatever amount of money they're willing to gamble. Read the correct response to the first statement. If the teachers answered correctly, they add the amount of money that they bet to their original $100; if they responded incorrectly, then they take *half* the amount of their bet and subtract it (it's nice to keep everyone in the game for awhile). At this point, everyone has a different amount of money to bet on the next response; some will have more than their initial $100, others less. Continue this process until all responses have been discussed, and end with a show of hands to find out how much money everyone has left; you might even award prizes to teachers with the greatest amounts of money.

Such playful gambling is an effective strategy for presenting background research information for the workshop topic, and it gives participants an opportunity to chat and share their expertise with one another.

Information to Include in the Opening

After beginning the workshop with an opening strategy that makes the participants take notice and sets the tone for the workshop, you will want to share some of the organizational details of the session. Within the first few minutes of the workshop, most participants like to have a sense of what specifically is going to happen. The information that facilitators include in the workshop introduction is generally similar, although it can be shared in a variety of ways. The amount of time this introduction takes depends upon the length of the workshop, but it should never take more than twenty minutes.

The Schedule/Agenda

In your introductory remarks, tell what you plan to talk about and outline a schedule for the workshop. Try to give details but make the schedule general enough to allow for some flexibility. Because the schedule is usually planned prior to the workshop, it needs to be open to incorporate additional information, unexpected events of the day, and topics related to the participants' needs. Schedules and agendas are important to help keep the workshop on course and increase the likelihood that you will accomplish your goals for the workshop. Participants, too, like to know what will occur during the workshop in order to organize the session in their own minds.

There are two types of schedules I use that seem to be appropriate for those teachers who want to know what is going to happen next yet allow me the flexibility I need.

TIME-BLOCK SCHEDULE

Breaks are important in any workshop, and people tend to remember that they will occur. Therefore, I often draw up a workshop schedule that is organized around break times. Although there is an announced ending time for the workshop, I do not specifically identify the close on the schedule. This gives me a little more leeway and allows me to read the participants to determine when it is time to stop.

A schedule for an all-day workshop about motivating students to read would look like the following:

Teaching Your Students to Love to Read

Beginning–Break	Motivating students to begin a book
Break–11:45	"Grabbers"—books students can't resist
11:45–1:00	Lunch
1:00–Break	Motivating students to continue to read using children's books in the curriculum
Break–End	Motivating students to read more books
	Surefire hits—books guaranteed to please

This schedule tells the teachers that a specific time is set aside for lunch but that other sessions are more flexible because of the broad topics identified.

AGENDA MAPS

Flowcharts can help participants visualize the agenda for the workshop by showing the flow of information and how the topics are related to each other. If the map is drawn on an overhead transparency, participants' special interests can easily be added. Figure 5.1 is an example of an agenda map for a workshop on using visuals.

Participant Responsibilities

Early in the introduction, I usually say that I have done the "work" of planning the day. The teachers' responsibility is to "shop" around for the insights, ideas, suggestions, and strategies that have the most relevance to them. Together we are a part of an effective "workshop." If there are any special guidelines for the day—things that participants will be expected to do or important details everyone needs to know—this is a good time to share that information as well.

Write the schedule you use for a typical day or class. One type of schedule would show specific topics and the time frame allotted for each topic:

9:05–9:10   Lunch count, attendance
9:10–9:20   Sharing

Another type of daily or class schedule would group the specific topics into broad categories and assign a time frame:

Beginning   Getting started
After beginning to middle of class   Reading and discussion of
                                      books
Last 15 minutes of class   Writing workshop

Write your daily schedule using both formats. Now examine the two different types of schedules to determine which can best be used as a model for your workshop schedule.

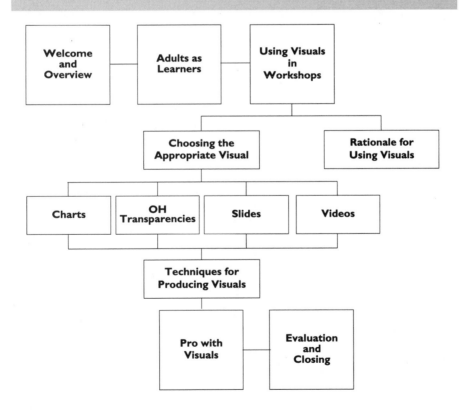

Figure 5.1 *Flowchart plan for conducting workshops*

Some workshop facilitators use a flip chart to show what they expect the participants to do; everyone can then see the list throughout the workshop. The list might include such things as

Be responsible for your own comfort.
Take responsibility for your own learning.
Stretch where you can.
Respect other participants' opinions and insights.
Share and become involved.

Facilitator's Goals and Participants' Expectations

During your introduction identify what you believe the participants will gain from the workshop; this will in turn help you determine whether your ideas match participants' expectations. Some participants want to know from the outset what they might learn in the workshop. Others will write the goals and aims as you share them and check them off as they are satisfied. Workshop facilitators sometimes list the predicted participant outcomes at the beginning of the workshop and use this list as a workshop organizer and a checkoff for participants.

> Write what you expect your students to do in your class in order to make school pleasant and successful for everyone. Then write all of the things you did as a participant in the most recent workshop you attended. Identify those items that appear on both lists. These may well be what the participants' responsibilities should be to enable them to get the most from your workshop.

For my workshops, however, I find very specific listings of aims to be too limiting. While predetermined goals can guide the workshop, some of the best results come about unexpectedly. To allow for and encourage this type of learning, I often present a minimum goal for the workshop and suggest that many participants will learn much more. I might say something like, "Each of you will leave this workshop with at least ten ideas you can use in your classroom, but many of you will learn even more. Most importantly, you will leave with ideas to renew your enthusiasm and your students' enthusiasm for reading." This statement provides a guideline but suggests the possibility of exceeding that goal. In a short workshop, you can find out participants' expectations somewhat informally, simply by asking whether the teachers have any other goals for the workshop or topics they would like to add to the agenda. A long workshop calls for more formalized techniques to identify participants' expectations, as described below.

QUESTIONS/ANSWERS

Teachers might be asked to write down questions they have about the topic of the workshop. In small groups they share their questions and determine the two that are the most important. The two questions from each group are written on chart paper and become the outline for the workshop. The workshop, then, will focus on the answers to the participants' questions. If you appropriately anticipated the needs of the teachers, most of the participants' questions will be directly related to the content you had already planned; in this question/answer strategy, the teachers basically reinforce what you had predetermined.

KNOW, WANT, LEARN—KWL

Another way to identify participants' expectations and do an informal needs assessment is to use a variation of the KWL strategy developed by Donna Ogle for use with students in the classroom (Carr and Ogle, 1987). Participants list what they *K*now about the topic, what they *W*ant to know, and what they anticipate *L*earning. (See KWL chart in the Appendix.) After teachers complete their individual KWL charts, they discuss them in small groups to identify any commonalities. The groups then share with one another the topics that seem to be of most interest, and these topics form the content of the workshop. Again, the "wants" from the teachers' lists will most likely reflect the content you had previously planned for the workshop. If the teachers raise issues you had not intended to address in the workshop, you can either adapt the content or tell participants that a particular topic will not be discussed. This gives them a chance to decide whether the workshop is going to meet their needs. This KWL strategy ties together the important components of the workshop—needs assessment (what the

To help you determine how to facilitate the section on participants' expectations in your workshop introduction, make a list of what you learned from the last workshop you attended. Under the heading "Expected Gains," list what you thought you would learn; under the heading "Unexpected Gains," list what you unexpectedly learned in that same workshop. Finally, make a list of what the facilitator proposed you would learn during the workshop under the heading "Facilitator Expectations." Compare these lists to help you decide how specific you want the expectation segment of your introduction to be. How open are your expectations to all types of learning?

teachers know), content (what the teachers want to know), and evaluation (what the teachers learned).

Facilitator's Introduction

Participants in the workshop want to know something about you. When you introduce yourself, include both your professional and personal background. Describe your professional connection with participants to emphasize your similarities and build bridges between you and the teachers attending your workshop. Share a personal experience related to the workshop topic to establish an informal rapport. I often use a set of transparencies with humorous graphics that illustrate the major joys and frustrations of both my personal and professional lives in order to give the participants a good sense of who I am.

Participants' Introduction

In a large group it isn't feasible for teachers to stand and introduce themselves individually. However, it is important for you and everyone else to know something about the people attending the workshop. At least ask for a show of hands indicating specific teaching or school positions, experience, and so on that influence the type of information the teachers will need from the workshop. It's always nice to acknowledge teachers for something special, such as most years as a classroom teacher. Ask questions that will help you predict how much the teachers know about the topic.

It is difficult, at first, to identify what you want and need to know about the workshop participants. Imagine that you walk into a room filled with classroom teachers. What would you like to know about them? Make a list of your curiosities that might include such things as the grade level or subject they teach, the number of students they have, the number of years they have taught, or their special teaching interests. After completing your list, star those items that you absolutely must know about the teachers at your workshop, and note briefly why that information is important. Put a question mark in front of those items it would be nice to know but you could probably conduct the workshop without knowing the information. Use these stars and question marks as a guide for planning the participant introduction segment of your workshop.

The purpose of the closing is to review the content of the workshop and to motivate the teachers to think about and implement the suggestions contained in the workshop. During the conclusion of the workshop, you'll want to summarize and highlight important concepts to reinforce participants' learning. You'll also want teachers to consider what they have learned during the workshop and how they will continue to learn about and use the information shared. At the same time, you want the teachers to leave with a sense that their time was well spent and with a strong motivation to further pursue the topic of the workshop. To accomplish all of these goals in the closing, there are some specific strategies you can use.

Make a final personal connection with the workshop participants. Remind them of the similarities that you share with them to reinforce the idea that if you can do it, so can they.

Make eye contact. Move around as you conclude, and consciously make eye contact with as many people as possible. Let the participants know that you care about them and are glad to have spent the workshop time with them.

Try to get a response from the participants. Encourage the participants to think about the workshop with feeling. A call to action, a humorous anecdote, an appeal to their sensitivities will have an impact and give the participants an emotional link to the workshop.

End on time. Eliminate whatever is necessary to assure that the teachers leave the workshop on or a little before the time the workshop is scheduled to end. Everyone is uncomfortable when a workshop runs long; people become more concerned about when the workshop will end than about what you are saying. For those who are anxious to leave, a late ending can negate what otherwise was an excellent workshop. Those who have questions or want additional information can always stay to talk with you after the workshop.

Closing Strategies

Many different strategies help to conclude the workshop with punch, to make it memorable. Some participants may only remember the conclusion, so do all that you can to make it worth recalling. Make the teachers feel good about the workshop and motivated to continue their learning. As with the introduction, relate the closing to the content of the workshop to help participants remember the context of the session.

Highlighting and Intensifying

Identify the key points of the workshop and their importance in the classroom. Remind the participants of the highlights so they feel assured that their time was well spent. You might say, for instance,"Today we talked about self-esteem and some specific strategies to encourage high self-esteem among your students. We've tried several strategies that you'll be able to use with your students. We only have to read the stories about rejected and abused people in our world to know the importance of the topic of self-esteem in our teaching." This type of closing provides a good summary that can solidify participants' recollections of their workshop experiences.

Call for Action

Refocus on the purpose of the workshop and ask for action. Give the teachers specific tasks that will implement the ideas, information, and strategies discussed during the workshop. After a workshop on encouraging reading, I've told participants, "Go back to your schools and, beginning tomorrow, give your students at least three opportunities a week to talk about their experiences with a book. Let them know the joy of reading a good book and sharing it with others." Many people need a concrete suggestion at the end of the workshop to get them started on putting the ideas into practice. Provide the teachers with that strategy.

Personal Anecdote

Share a personal experience that illuminates how the content of the workshop has affected your life. Here's an anecdote I've used in my reading workshop:

> We've talked a lot today about strategies to extend students' experiences with a favorite book. I remember the first time my mother took a stone and put it in the bottom of a pan of water on the stove and made stone soup. I wasn't very old at the time, but I was old enough to know that you didn't get soup from a stone. That day, in our kitchen, my mother and I recreated the story as she asked me for additional ingredients that would make the stone soup even tastier. That truly was the best soup I had ever eaten, and from that day, whenever we had soup (even the kind in a can), there was a stone in the bottom of the pan. Stone Soup by Marcia Brown is still one of my favorite books—because of the story, certainly, but also because of the extended experience my mother and I had with the story. I truly believe that my love for books (and food) began on that rainy afternoon in the kitchen with my mother, the soup, and a wonderful story. Your students deserve to have the same kind of experience with their favorite stories, and you deserve to see the results of those experiences.

A personal testimonial to the impact of the strategies shared in the workshop provides extra motivation for the teachers to implement what they've learned.

Participants' Commitments

Ask participants to write one action they are committed to taking as a result of attending your workshop. Volunteers can share their commitments, one right after another, so everyone can hear what others plan to do:

- "I'm going to read aloud to my students every day, at different times, for a total of at least twenty minutes."
- "I'm going to compliment at least three students about something unrelated to their schoolwork during each class."
- "I'm going to use the overhead projector for instruction in one new way before the end of the month."
- "I'm going to include a novel in my next history unit."

Not only does this focus the participants' attention on concrete action, it also serves as a review; someone may well be committed to doing something about a topic that some other participant had entirely forgotten.

Last Laugh

Everyone likes to laugh, and humor provides an upbeat, effective end to the workshop. A story I sometimes use to close a workshop about books that includes extensive bibliographies actually happened to me:

About a month after I had completed a workshop about books and reading, I had a telephone call from one of the participants. This person was more than a little irate with me because she had ordered every book on my bibliography and there was one *that she didn't like. Can you believe it? Only* one! *I think that's pretty good! Read the books listed on your bibliographies to see if you can find the* one *you don't like.*

If participants leave with a chuckle, they will remember the workshop as positive and may be further inclined to apply its content.

Provocative Statements and Statistics

Surprise the participants with a statement that will give them something to promote their thought and inquiry into the workshop topic long after the session is over:

We have talked this afternoon about the latest books for children, focusing on the quality and how to use them to motivate kids to read. However, a recent article in The Atlantic *suggests that books written for children are not what they used to be. The author implies that even some of the best authors for children are writing for the money and sacrificing the story. He advocates that it is much more beneficial for children to watch television than read the literature that is written today. What do you think?*

An unexpected statement in the closing offers participants a structure in which to place their thoughts about the workshop. They will review the workshop information as they identify evidence and ideas that either support or invalidate the statement.

And Now, One More Story

Let a talented writer write the closing for your workshop. Find a really good story or poem that sums up the point you were making. At the conclusion of a workshop for parents about reading and books for their children, I often share *Fix-It!* by David McPhail. In this story the author successfully shows that a good book can succeed in bringing pleasure to a child when all else has failed. McPhail reinforces the point of the workshop with his delightful story and wonderful illustrations. Begin a collection of stories and poems that support the content of your workshop; such materials can help you increase the impact of your message.

Action Plans

Just before the end of the workshop, the teachers can complete an action plan that indicates specifically how they are going to apply something they learned in the workshop. By writing down what they will be doing, they may internalize the process needed to move the workshop ideas into reality. The plan might look something like this:

1. Idea that I want to implement:
2. Benefits of implementing this idea:
3. Potential problems associated with implementing this idea:
4. Possible solutions for each of the problems associated with implementing this idea:
5. Resources that can be used to implement this idea:
6. Date by which I hope to have idea implemented:
7. Celebration planned when idea is implemented:

Remind the teachers that in order for their action plans to be successful, they must be realistic. The idea must be workable and important to them because of the positive change it will bring about.

Winning Ideas

During your workshop participants will hear about and think of many ideas. Encourage them to categorize and rate the ideas by identifying the suggestions that are deserving of each of these "awards": Most Practical, Easiest to Implement, Most Interesting, Most Promising, Most Creative, Biggest Surprise, Most Thought-Provoking, and Overall Best. After completing their lists individually, teachers can compare their prize-winning ideas. This strategy, like others, serves as a review of the approaches suggested throughout the workshop.

Again, remember that it is important that the closing of your workshop is effective not only on the logical level but on an emotional level as well. Take care of any last-minute issues or reminders and then close with a final element that elicits an emotional reaction to leave the participants with a powerful feeling about the workshop itself—and with good feelings about implementing the workshop content.

In Conclusion

The beginning and ending of your workshop are its two most important elements: the beginning sets the tone for the session, and the ending determines to a great extent the feelings the teachers will carry away from the workshop. You should, then, plan these segments very carefully. By following the guidelines and using some of the strategies suggested in this chapter, you can increase the likelihood that your workshop will both start off right and conclude on a successful note.

Works Cited and Suggested Readings

Berry, S. E.; and Garmston, R. J. "Become a State of the Art Presenter."
   Training and Development Journal (January 1987): 19–23

Brookfield, Stephen. *Developing Critical Thinkers.* San Francisco: Jossey-
   Bass, 1987

————. *The Skillful Teacher.* Chapter 3. San Francisco: Jossey-Bass, 1990

————. "Using Critical Incidents to Explore Learners' Assumptions." In
   *Fostering Critical Reflection in Adulthood: A Guide to Transformative and
   Emancipatory Learning,* edited by Jack Mezirow and Associates. San
   Francisco: Jossey-Bass, 1990

Carr, Eileen; and Ogle, Donna. "K-W-L Plus: A Strategy for Comprehension
   and Summarization." *Journal of Reading,* 30 (April 1987)

Clair, Joan; Hoffman, Connie; and Olson, Judy. *Getting It Started, Keeping It Going, Wrapping It Up.* Federal Way, WA: VISTA Associates, 1990

Corbett, Adele H. "Give Participants Responsibility for Learning: Techniques for Opening a Workshop." *Journal of Staff Development,* 13 (Winter 1992): 40–42

Davis, Larry Nolan. *Planning, Conducting, and Evaluating Workshops.* Austin, TX: Learning Concepts, 1974

Garmston, Robert. "Notes on the Persuasive Art of Presenting: Openers." *Developer* (December 1990/January 1991): 3,7

Hamlin, Sonya. *How to Talk So People Listen.* Chapter 5. New York: Harper & Row, 1988

Hanks, Kurt; and Pulsipher, Gerreld. *Getting Your Message Across.* Los Altos, CA: Crisp, 1991

Mandel, Steve. *Effective Presentation Skills.* Sections 6 and 7. Los Altos, CA: Crisp, 1987

Moffett, Cerylle; and Warger, Cynthia. *The Human Resource Development Program Handbook: A Practical Guide for Staff Developers.* Part 2. Alexandria, VA: Association for Supervision and Curriculum Development, 1988

Pike, Robert W. *Creative Training Techniques Handbook.* Chapters 3 and 4. Minneapolis, MN: Lakewood Books, 1989

Smith, Duane, ed. *Creative Training Techniques: A Newsletter of Tips, Tactics, and How-Tos for Delivering Effective Training,* 3 (May 1990): 8

6

Selecting and Presenting Workshop Content

Robert Garmston and Bruce Wellman (1992) suggest that up to 70 percent of the impact of a message can be attributed to the manner in which it is delivered. Their assessment highlights the importance of having an effective way to share the information in your workshop. After you have identified the topic, you need to determine the information you want to include in the workshop and how to present it.

Determining the Content of the Workshop

As you think about your workshop, you need to consider not only what information you want to include but why the teachers need to know the information. The content of the workshop is the reason for its being. That content needs to be clear in your mind before the workshop begins and clear to the participants when the workshop is over.

Most facilitators deliberately plan too much content for their workshops. Don't expect to be able to share all that you want in the workshop, and don't consider it a major problem if you don't get to everything you had planned. It is usually better to have too much content and have to decide what not to use than to have insufficient content and try to make up something to add. You need to remember to keep the amount of content in the workshop realistic. Because you are familiar with the content, you have probably forgotten the complexities involved in what you are sharing. Too much too fast can be very difficult for those who are just learning the ideas.

I've generally found that it takes twice as long to do something during the workshop than I originally supposed. Simplify the decision of what to include and what to leave out by identifying those points and support that have to be included, those that should be included, and those that it would simply be nice to include. I use an exclamation point to mark the "must-haves," an asterisk for the "should-haves," and a bullet for the "nice-to-haves." As the workshop progresses, use your clock to help you determine how many of the lower-priority items need to be eliminated.

Another way to evaluate the content is to prioritize what the participants must know at the end of the workshop, what would be good for them to know, what would be nice for them to know, and what they really do not need to know.

> Think about the last workshop you attended. Identify its topic and list the points the facilitator introduced during the workshop. From your perspective as a participant, rank the points as those that had to be included (!), those that should be included (*), those that were nice to have included (•), and those points that were questionably included (?). Think about how you made those judgments and use those same guidelines as you prioritize your own workshop content.

Organizing the Workshop Content

The content sequence of the workshop needs to make sense to the participants who are not as familiar with the topic as you are. It may be appropriate to share this sequence and sketch out for them what material you will cover first to make subsequent material understandable. Another organizational scheme might involve rotating various types of ideas: a quiet idea, a reflective idea, an idea with pizzazz, another quiet idea, another reflective idea, and so on.

Putting the content into a usable workshop model can be confusing. Write your content ideas down so you can see them, then continue to evaluate and eliminate ideas to develop a well-organized workshop. In planning a workshop, I use two different processes that provide a framework in which I can consider all workshop content possibilities.

Mindmapping

A mindmap is helpful in showing you what you want to include in the workshop and how it all fits together. It is a nonlinear, brainstorming strategy in which similar ideas are clustered together.

There are certain fundamentals to follow when you develop a mindmap:

Begin with the main idea, a nucleus word, printed in the center
of a clean page.
Draw a circle around the main idea.
Write down key words that relate to the main idea.

Keep the ideas free flowing.

Don't try to put ideas in specific places on the map initially.

Use the same color of line to connect related ideas.

Go back and add ideas; don't expect (or try) to complete the
map in one sitting.

Try using pictures and other drawings to provide visual clues.

Label subtopics related to the original idea.

A mindmap I used for this handbook appears in Figure 6.1.

Figure 6.1 *Mindmap*

Everyone has taken notes during a presentation or class that were impossible to interpret later. The next time you want to take notes, use the mindmapping strategy. Instead of trying to develop the standard linear outline, select key words and identify connections as the presentation continues. At the conclusion of the session, add any details that you think will make the connections easier to understand. A few days later, look at your mindmap. Does it help you to remember the content of the presentation? If so, try organizing your workshop using this technique. If not, try a more linear organizational strategy.

The Flexible Outline

This planning strategy is similar to a linear outline but allows you to move topics around easily as you consider and reconsider your workshop content. Using self-adhesive notes, jot down the ideas you want to include in your workshop, putting one idea on each note. Arrange the notes into broad categories. If you have an idea that doesn't fit with anything else, determine whether the idea is important enough to have a category of its own. Eliminate ideas that overlap. Keep arranging, rearranging, and evaluating until you have the two to five main ideas you want to include in your workshop.

On larger self-stick tags, write each of the main ideas. Arrange the smaller notes as subcategories underneath the categories. Try different arrangements until you find the one that makes the most sense. At the conclusion of this process, you will have a linear outline to follow as you move into your next step of planning.

Sharing the Workshop Content

As you decide how to organize and deliver the content of the workshop, consider how you teach your students.

Before participants in the workshop can try an idea or strategy, they need to know a certain amount of information. There are a number of techniques to share this new information. In this handbook I focus on the two strategies that are generally the easiest and most reliable for beginners: lectures and

> Write the plan for a lesson that has been especially successful with your students. Be very specific and list all components of the lesson, including such things as:
>
> - anticipated learning outcome
> - motivation for learning
> - materials used
> - instructional techniques
>   - what the teacher did
>   - what the students did
> - modeling
> - reinforcement
> - evaluation
>
> This lesson can be your initial guide for planning your workshop. Motivate, describe, and model before asking teachers to try the activity, just as you would motivate, describe, and model with your students in the classroom.

presentations and brainstorming. Other effective instructional strategies, such as role-plays and simulations, are more complex and require some comfort with ambiguity that many beginning workshop facilitators do not yet have.

Lectures and Presentations

When new information is called for or when familiar material needs to be reorganized, lectures and presentations are often the best means of raising the awareness and readiness of participants. Presentations to the total group can give the participants a common knowledge base as well as a shared experience. Although they may put learners into a passive role, when delivered with enthusiasm, energy, and passion, such presentations are an effective strategy for exposing people to ideas they had not previously considered. In fact, although lectures do not appeal to the full range of human senses, adults do sometimes prefer this teaching strategy.

Successful presenters and lecturers are usually enthusiastic, lively, and organized, keeping the presentation of information relatively short or punctuating it by discussions and audience response points. They bring in personal examples to validate the points and may shift the activities in the workshop from facilitator to participants and back again every ten to twenty minutes.

Group Brainstorming

Brainstorming either generates new ideas or elaborates upon content being discussed. It establishes the link between the participants' own experience and the content of the workshop, and it is most effective when information and ideas can best be obtained from the participants themselves. It encourages participants to think creatively and to expand upon each other's ideas. The goal is to have the group produce the greatest number of ideas possible on a given topic within a limited amount of time. Three basic rules for brainstorming are that all ideas suggested are accepted and recorded, no criticism of any idea is allowed, and everyone must share any idea that seems even remotely connected to the topic. The real key to productive brainstorming sessions is knowing when to stop—before the participants lose their enthusiasm, while the ideas are still flowing.

A couple of adaptations for brainstorming have been particularly helpful to me. One is to eliminate the expected responses by identifying them before the brainstorming begins: "I know three reasons why you're attending this workshop. I know that you're here to learn some ideas you can use with your students. I know you're here because the content is of interest to you. And I know you're here because you need a day away from your students. Now, what are

You have probably used the brainstorming strategy in your classroom. Drawing upon this experience with your students, list some of the adaptations you have developed to make the brainstorming session more effective. Consider which of these adaptations would be appropriate to use with adults as well.

some other reasons for your being here?" By doing this, I avoid taking up valuable time listening to the usual responses.

Another adaptation I sometimes use is to begin with silent brainstorming. Everyone first makes an individual list of ideas related to the topic. Each person contributes one idea from the personal list to begin the brainstorming session. Then everyone adds new ideas, many of which have been inspired by what was shared from the personal lists.

Additional Considerations in Sharing Content

Whatever strategy you select for sharing content, you should keep in mind some additional guidelines from experienced facilitators.

Hook the participants with a motivating, practical idea at the beginning. If teachers attend your workshop because they want to learn information and ideas they can use in their classrooms, then start off by giving them an idea they can adapt and use with students of various ages. This practical tip will set the stage for a workshop jam-packed with helpful ideas, and the teachers will be eager to hear more. A good idea will also quickly establish your credibility.

Present one idea at a time, and give participants an opportunity to process the information. Be certain that participants have an understanding of one idea before you share another. Give them an opportunity to think about, question, review, try out, or otherwise react to the idea through visual examples, group interaction, or a specific exercise. Too much information without time for processing and reflection can lead to information overload. Some facilitators suggest that for every ten to twenty minutes of facilitator sharing, there should be two to ten minutes of interaction. This formula does illustrate the importance of variety but can also lead to a boring routine. See the chapter on interactive strategies for some ideas you can use to help teachers process workshop information.

Be specific. Provide lots of relevant examples and illustrations. Put the content into the specific contexts of the participants. Avoid generalizations and broad questions.

Demonstrate, then activate. Many times it will be appropriate for you to model an activity for participants before asking them to do it for themselves. This gives them a clear idea of the task presented and answers many of their process questions. Be careful, though, not to model those activities in which you want to receive participants' insights; your demonstration may lead them to a particular way of thinking.

Review often during the workshop. Participants must be reminded about what is being said. When we are reading a book, we can flip back to verify what we previously read. During a workshop participants cannot flip back for a quick recap, so it is critical that the facilitator provide reviews to help participants organize their thoughts and prepare for upcoming information. A facilitator might say, for example,

We have just discussed the five things that teachers can do that students indicate are most effective in motivating them to read: read the first few pages, describe settings where stories take place, talk about books students have read, talk about lives of authors, and read aloud a chapter from a book every day. Now let's look at how we can use this information in designing strategies to get our students excited about books.

Tell participants the value of the workshop content. Remind the teachers of the importance of the information and ideas they are learning in the workshop and how they can implement everything in their classrooms. Give them plenty of opportunities to consider the potential of what they are learning, allowing them to discuss their own experiences. Help them see the benefits and value of the workshop in as many ways as possible.

Allow for unexpected learning. Not all of the effective learning in a workshop is the planned learning. Don't overstructure the session so that there is no time or chance for digressions and other unpredictable turns that could lead to additional learning.

Supporting What You Say

Teachers need to know why what you are suggesting is important for them to understand, implement, or think about. Unless you give specific support for your ideas, some participants may discount all of what you have to say.

Figures and Statistics

Find and use numbers to represent and reinforce the facts you present. In the workshop on reading, for instance, the facilitator might tell the participants, "Twenty percent of Americans cannot name the title of a book they want to read" or, "The average time a student spends reading outside of school is three to five minutes." Be certain that the numbers you use are up-to-date and have not been refuted by another source.

Facts

Statements about realities that can be verified by third-party accounts or direct observation will support what you are asserting. Use the teachers' realities when presenting a point by appealing to their classroom experience: "We are all well aware of the impact that divorce has had on the students we teach. What are some of the things we know to be true?" Teachers will relate to and confirm a fact such as this because of their own experiences.

Definitions

Clarifying your terminology helps everyone to follow your message and helps ascertain that everyone is starting with the same understanding. You may point out that there are many definitions of a term, then give the definition that describes *your* usage. Simultaneous projection of a transparency of the definition will further support your explanation.

Anecdotes

Use stories from your own classroom experiences to illustrate a point.

> *I know the benefits of reading aloud to students. I had one student who was an excellent reader but never chose to read a book. Whenever I read aloud, though, he sat right in front, in rapt attention. One day I asked him why he never liked to read books himself if he so obviously enjoyed it when I read books aloud. He looked at me incredulously and said, "But you take the bore* out of reading."

Examples and Illustrations

Share student work with teachers to show that the idea you're suggesting is effective. Teachers like to see what students have done to help them gauge the feasibility of applying the ideas in their own classrooms. Bring examples from students of all abilities to honestly portray the effectiveness of the idea.

Authorities and Experts

Use specific people, places, and dates when providing support for your ideas. Try to find names of people your participants will recognize. In a program about the reading and writing connection, you might quote from Katherine Paterson's book *The Gates of Excellence:* "The writer does not

Keep a journal and file of classroom experiences, situations, and copies of student work that are poignant and thought-provoking. Concentrate on those that other teachers will be able to relate to and those that are especially humorous or sensitive. Collect not only the successes but also the failures— examples of student work that, for some reason, didn't turn out as you had hoped— for increased credibility. Use these examples and anecdotes as workshop support.

pass through the gates of excellence alone but in the company of readers" (p. 14). Supporting information is often remembered longer than the original point, so be certain it is accurate, up-to-date, easy-to-understand, and relevant.

In Conclusion

As you're selecting and planning how to present the content of the workshop, apply your classroom experience. As in your classroom, your confidence will increase if you have too much rather than too little content. When you organize your content, use the same strategies that go into lesson planning. In this chapter we examined two strategies for sharing content—lectures and presentations and group brainstorming—as well as the importance of backup material for the statements you make. Remember that how the content is shared usually makes the difference between an exceptional workshop and a merely acceptable one.

Works Cited and Suggested Readings

Berry, S. E., and Garmston, R. J. "Become a State of the Art Presenter." *Training and Development Journal* (January 1987): 19–23

Bocchino, Rob. "Using Mind Mapping as a Note-Taking Tool." *Developer* (March 1991): 1–4

Boyle, Patrick G. *Planning Better Programs.* Chapter 16. New York: McGraw-Hill, 1981

Brookfield, Stephen. *The Skillful Teacher.* Chapter 3. San Francisco: Jossey-Bass, 1990

Buzan, Tony. *Using Both Sides of Your Brain.* New York: E. P. Dutton, 1983

Draves, William A. *How to Teach Adults.* Manhattan, KS: Learning Resources Network, 1984

Garmston, Robert J. "The Persuasive Art of Presenting: What Content Is Most Important?" *Journal of Staff Development,* 13 (Spring 1992): 46–47

———. "Taming the Content/Process Teeter-Totter." *Journal of Staff Development,* 13 (Winter 1992): 50–51

Garmston, Robert J.; and Wellman, Bruce. *How to Make Presentations That Teach and Transform.* Alexandria, VA: Association for Supervision and Curriculum Development, 1992

Hamlin, Sonya. *How to Talk So People Listen.* Chapter 7. New York: Harper & Row, 1988

Hanks, Kurt; and Pulsipher, Gerreld. *Getting Your Message Across.* Los Altos, CA: Crisp, 1991

Knowles, Malcolm S. *The Modern Practice of Adult Education: From Pedagogy to Andragogy.* 2d ed. Chapter 8. New York: Cambridge, 1980

Knox, Alan B. *Helping Adults Learn.* Chapters 5 and 8. San Francisco: Jossey-Bass, 1987

———. "Helping Teachers Help Adults Learn." In *Teaching Adults Effectively.* San Francisco: Jossey-Bass, 1980

Paterson, Katherine. *The Gates of Excellence.* New York: E. P. Dutton, 1981

Pike, Robert W. *Creative Training Techniques Handbook.* Chapter 2. Minneapolis, MN: Lakewood Books, 1989

Powers, Bob. *Instructor Excellence: Mastering the Delivery of Training.* Chapters 5 and 8. San Francisco: Jossey-Bass, 1992

Rico, Gabriele Lusser. *Writing the Natural Way.* Los Angeles: J. P. Tarcher, 1983

Seaman, Don F.; and Fellenz, Robert A. *Effective Strategies for Teaching Adults.* Chapter 3. Columbus, OH: Merrill, 1989

Smith, Terry C. *Making Successful Presentations: A Self-Teaching Guide.* 2d ed. Chapter 4. New York: John Wiley & Sons, 1991

Sorcinelli, Gino; and Sorcinelli, Mary Deane. "The Lecture in an Adult Education Environment: Teaching Strategies." *Lifelong Learning,* 10 (January 1987): 8–10

Westmeyer, Paul. *Effective Teaching in Adult and Higher Education.* Chapter 4. Springfield, IL: Charles C. Thomas, 1988

7

Workshop Packets and Materials

Teachers like workshop packets and materials, often citing high-quality materials as one characteristic of an effective workshop. Many teachers like to have something concrete to reinforce and remind them of their workshop learning and activities. Well-chosen and well-prepared workshop materials will do this.

Workshop Packet Content

Pages in workshop packets are designed for a number of different reasons as discussed below.

Informational Materials

Some of your workshop materials will reinforce important ideas in the workshop by restating and supplementing the workshop content. Figure 7.1, for example, shows a page that would be included in a packet for a reading workshop. It gives additional information that supports the inclusion of author studies in a reading program. This type of information is not necessarily presented during the workshop but could be of interest to the participants later.

Use your own experience and expertise when preparing your handouts. Make a list of what you like about the materials you receive from workshops that you attend. Consider specifically the content, use, format, quantity, and quality of the packet.

Summary Materials

Some handouts will summarize main topics of the workshop and will be used both during the workshop and as a reference for teachers after the workshop is over, when they share with others what they learned. Figure 7.2 is a sample summary, indicating the main ideas presented in a workshop on library programs.

Fill-in Materials

Teachers will complete certain handouts as a workshop activity. During a reading workshop, for instance, they might fill in an acronym such as the one in Figure 7.3.

MEET THE AUTHOR

It's Time to Return the Author to Reading

- **Reading is an interactive process**
  Reading takes into account the reader's knowledge, intentions, and energies. What isn't accounted for, however, is the author, the other person involved in this interactive process. Students need to know that the book has been written by an author, and that authors write for a purpose; students need to be aware of the intent involved when the author writes a book.

- **Good readers think about an author's intent**
  When good readers become confused by text, they try to understand the author's intent; understanding why the author included a passage helps to resolve differences in interpretation.

- **Good readers seek out specific authors**
  It is reassuring for readers to seek out a recognized voice and watch the author grow. Studies have shown that those readers who seek out multiple books by the same authors are the best readers in terms of reading comprehension.

- **Reading comprehension improves when readers are encouraged to think about the author**
  Studies show that the best readers are those who are involved in author awareness activities. When readers think about why authors write, they can better understand the author's intent. Increased awareness that authors write to communicate helps readers better understand the social interaction that is reading.

MEET THE AUTHOR

PEGGY A. SHARP-page 2

Figure 7.1
*Informational
handout*

Some workshop materials should stand on their own, but it's a good idea to include several that need your explanation in order for the reader fully to understand their message. After all, you want to make certain that there is a reason for teachers to take part in your workshop, that they can't get all of the information from the handouts alone.

Supporting Materials

Additional information that is not specifically addressed during the workshop but that supports its content will be the focus of certain materials. Figure 7.4 shows a handout designed for a workshop on reading.

Ideas to Try

Some materials will contain ready-to-use strategies for the classroom based upon the content of the workshop but not specifically described in the session.

Figure 7.5 is an example of a classroom activity that teachers can try out to stimulate writing. Similar—though not identical—activities would have been presented in the workshop.

Organizing the Workshop Packet

The materials from the workshop need to be organized for easy access both during the workshop and afterward.

Crediting Yourself

Include the title of the workshop and your name and phone number on every page of workshop material that is not bound into a booklet. This provides the teachers with quick access to you if they have questions after the workshop and also reminds them where they received the information. Parts of your workshop packet will probably be photocopied and given to others—a compli-

STRENGTHENING YOUR LIBRARY PROGRAM

Roles of the Library Specialist

✔ **Instructional Consultant**
☐ Selects, evaluates, and uses resources and emerging technologies.
☐ Participates in the process of curriculum development.
☐ Designs, produces, implements, and evaluates instructional units.
☐ Collaborates with classroom teachers and instructional leaders within the school.
☐ Assesses the potential impact of emerging information and instructional technologies on the school program.

✔ **Teacher**
☐ Instructs students in skills, knowledge, and attitudes concerning information access, use, evaluation, and production of library media resources.
☐ Instructs educators in selection, use, evaluation, and production of library media resources.
☐ Instructs parents in sharing, reading, listening, and viewing experiences with children.

✔ **Information Specialist**
☐ Provides flexible access to the library media center.
☐ Provides adequate resources to meet changing needs of the school's instructional programs.
☐ Assists students in locating information and developing search strategy skills.
☐ Assists users in selecting appropriate resources.
☐ Establishes flexible policies for use of resources, emphasizing maximum access to all users.
☐ Provides retrieval systems for accurate and efficient access to information resources.

PEGGY A. SHARP-page 7

Figure 7.2
*Summary
handout*

TEACHING YOUR STUDENTS TO LOVE TO READ

**60 Second Strategy or
I Need a Good Book . . . Fast**

C OVER
A UTHOR
N UMBER OF PAGES

I LLUSTRATIONS
T

B
E

F
O
R

M
E

Figure 7.3
Fill-in handout

PEGGY A. SHARP- page 4

ment on your ideas. If your name is on each page, your name is likelier to be associated with your ideas.

Page Numbers

Number each page of materials. If you are going to distribute the pages in a pocket folder, number the pages at the top for easy visibility. If the pages are to be combined into a packet that is either stapled or bound in some manner, numbers at the bottom of the page are easier to spot. Throughout the session, refer to the page numbers on the materials so that teachers can follow along with the presentation.

Sections

Color coding different sections of your materials helps participants quickly find pages relating to different sections of the workshop. Different colors of paper can significantly increase the time and cost of collation, however.

Always include some space in the handouts on which teachers can take necessary notes relating to the particular page. Also identify a couple of pages as appropriate for notes only. Include section pages that signify a change of major topic area and a table of contents to help teachers access the materials after the workshop. (For additional information on the design of your workshop packets, the section on visuals in Chapter 9 includes suggestions that would be appropriate for your printed page as well.)

To Bind or Not to Bind?

Books carry a lot of credibility, and workshop materials that are bound into a booklet seem to have more authority than loose pieces of paper. However, unless you plan to present the same workshop for many, many people, the cost of binding the materials into a stapled book may be prohibitive. Many school districts and quick-print shops have thermobind machines that can give your materials a booklike appearance relatively inexpensively. If you intend for the teachers to copy the handouts, put the papers into a folder. Whatever method of organization you choose for your materials, be sure to include a cover sheet with the name, location, and date of the workshop, along with your name, address, and telephone number as its facilitator.

TEACHING READING WITH LITERATURE

Why Aren't You Using the Workbooks?

1. **Skills instruction should look as much like the reading act as possible.**
   Jerome Harste, Carolyn Burke, and Virginia Woodward, *Children, Their Language, and World: Initial Encounters with Print*, 1981.

2. **Children need to see the connections between word attack instruction and creating meaning when they read.**
   Barbara Taylor and Linda Nosbush, "Oral Reading for Meaning: A Technique for Improving Work Identification Skills," *The Reading Teacher*, 1983.

3. **The only justification for phonics instruction is to help readers construct meaning when they read.**
   Terry Johnson and Daphne R. Louis, *Literacy Through Literature*, 1987.

4. **The time to teach skills is when children are experimenting with language and are both interested in and need such instruction.**
   Frank May, *Reading as Communication: An Interactive Approach*, 1986.

5. **The reading process needs to be honored during skills instruction.**
   Daniel Hittleman, *Developmental Reading, K–8, Teaching from a Whole Language Perspective*, 1988.

PEGGY A. SHARP-page I

Figure 7.4
Supporting material handout

It's usually preferable to give the workshop materials to the participants as they enter the room. This lets the teachers glance through them prior to the workshop and begin focusing on the topic. When participants have the workshop packet during the presentation you can refer to specific pages.

Distribute materials during a workshop only when it is absolutely necessary. I only give out materials during the workshop when it is important that the teachers not see the material prior to its use, and then I distribute the papers as quickly as possible. There's no reason to give participants anything that will compete with what you have to say. If you do hand out materials for review, be sure to allow enough time for reading, so you're not trying to talk while people are trying to read.

Avoid handing out materials at the conclusion of the workshop. Some facilitators may try this as an incentive for people to stay, but if teachers are sitting through a workshop only to get the materials, they have probably missed the

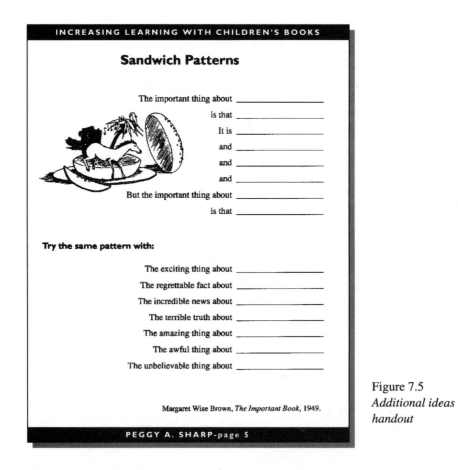

Figure 7.5
*Additional ideas
handout*

point of the program anyway. Without having the materials during the presentation, teachers do not know what they should be writing down and what is included in the handout, and they may be annoyed at having to take unnecessary notes. The deluge of people trying to pick up the materials at the end of the session can also be frustrating. Teachers in your workshop deserve better than that.

In Conclusion

Workshop materials and packets are the concrete reminder of your program. Because you want these materials to reinforce both the workshop content and experience, make them as clear, concise, practical, and appealing as possible. These handouts should be as useful after the workshop as they were during the session. Well-designed and -developed materials will remind the teachers of a carefully planned and effectively facilitated workshop.

Works Cited and Suggested Readings

Eastman Kodak Company. *Copy Preparation.* Rochester, NY: Eastman Kodak, 1977

————. *Graphic Design.* Rochester, NY: Eastman Kodak, 1977

————. *Photography and Layout for Reproduction.* Rochester, NY: Eastman Kodak, 1977

Ellington, H. *Producing Teaching Materials: A Handbook for Teachers and Trainers.* New York: Nichols, 1985

Jonassen, D. H. *The Technology of Text.* Englewood Cliffs, NJ: Educational Technology Publications, 1982

Raines, Claire. *Visual Aids in Business.* Section 3. Los Altos, CA: Crisp, 1989

8

Involvement and Interactive Strategies

Education is a give-and-take activity in which both the teacher and learner bring values and ideas to the learning situation. In order to reap the benefits of a workshop, participants need to become engaged in a workshop by caring about the content and assuming responsibility for their own learning. Additional involvement can be encouraged, however, through interactive strategies that provide opportunities for workshop participants to share their experience, insights, and ideas with others. The strategies can motivate participants to reflect on their experiences and to try out their new ideas on others who have a common background. This involvement—be it talking to a partner, working in small groups, or brainstorming before the large group—is a key to a successful workshop.

Increasing Involvement in the Workshop

Teacher involvement in the workshop doesn't happen just because the facilitator wants it. There are certain things you can do, however, to increase the likelihood that teachers will become actively involved in a workshop.

Explain why participants might need to attend the workshop. Teachers usually want to know what's in it for them, so it is up to the facilitator to explain what that is. I often explicitly describe a scenario with which they are all familiar (students who do not seem interested in learning a new math skill, for example) and tell them how the workshop will provide them with some suggestions for changing the situation.

Remind participants that they are responsible for their own learning. You can't require the teachers to learn during the workshop; you can only provide them with an opportunity to learn. Encourage the teachers to think about their expectations for the workshop and what they're willing to do to reach those expectations. At the beginning of the workshop, I often ask teachers to write down what they hope to get from their attendance and then to list three things they can do to help themselves get that information. If participants set individual goals, it tends to help them buy into the program.

Include practical applications in the workshop. Many participants want to know how the presentation will affect them. By sharing examples that show how you and other teachers have used the ideas and information, you will help the participants understand how they can put the ideas to work. I usually bring samples of student work so that teachers can see how to carry through with the suggestions. I may also ask teachers to do the activity I am demonstrating, so that they get a sense of how is done.

Establish a learning environment of mutual respect, trust, helpfulness, and acceptance. Teachers need to know that their questions and suggestions will be accepted and regarded in the spirit in which they are given. Make it clear that their ideas are valid and will be respected. Involvement will increase to the extent that the participants feel they can trust one another and will not be attacked or disregarded because of their opinions.

Ask for and respond to participant input throughout the day. Teachers have specific ideas about content, time allocations, learning activities, and other aspects of the workshop. Use their input, both verbal and nonverbal, to determine how much time to spend on an activity, topics to include or omit, and so on. I usually present an overview of the content of the workshop in the initial stages of the session. I always make it clear, however, that the overview is tentative and can easily be adapted to participants' needs and interests.

Acknowledge, recognize, and encourage participation in the workshop. Make it clear that you know that everyone has expertise to share, and give the teachers opportunities to do so. If during a break a participant makes a valuable comment related to the content of the workshop, share that remark with the rest of the group when the group comes back together. When someone tells you how she or he has used a particular idea, encourage the person to tell everyone in the group about it.

Involve the group when you answer individual questions. If someone has a particular question, ask others in the group for their solutions. The more people involved in the answer, the more will be interested in the question.

Encourage interpersonal relationships in the workshop. Allow the teachers a chance to meet and talk with one another and with you, the facilitator. Have plenty of breaks, and encourage people to have lunch with someone new or introduce themselves to someone they don't know. Make yourself available before the workshop, during breaks, and after the session to talk with participants on an interpersonal level. Participation will likely increase as the teachers feel a greater sense of group cohesiveness and concern for the workshop.

Encourage the participants to mix during the workshop. It is usually most convenient for teachers to work with those sitting near them. However, there may be times when teachers of the same grade levels or who teach the same subject need to work together, or when those who have different positions within the school should team up. Identify different groups for various activities. If you mix the participants, people will not feel shut out by cliques that may form. Almost any criteria can be used to designate groups, such as those mentioned in the "Geographically Speaking" and "I'm Like a . . ." activities in the icebreaker section of this chapter.

Provide opportunities for small group, partner, and large group participation. Some adults are shy about speaking before a large group but are more than willing to share their good ideas with a much smaller group. Give them the chance to participate on several levels, from interacting with just a few other participants to speaking to the group as a whole.

Provide activities that generate success. Teachers need to feel a certain sense of accomplishment if they are going to continue to participate. Develop strategies that assure success to help everyone feel competent.

Give clear directions for group activities. Teachers will enjoy group activities more if they are not confused and anxious about what to do next. Put directions on the overhead projector or on chart paper to help participants remember the specific sequence of their group activities.

Assign group members specific roles. Generate enthusiasm for the activity by assigning the various roles using an element of surprise:

- Ask someone in each group to volunteer to do something. Then tell them they have volunteered to find the group leaders—the people seated to their right.
- Make the person with the largest family the recorder.
- Make the person from the smallest high school graduating class the motivator.
- Assign the person with the least number of letters in his or her name the task of encouraging the group.
- Give the job of speaker to the person with the smallest feet.
- Let the person who returns to the group last after the break be the leader.

Share the criteria first, then identify the role for the person who meets each criterion.

Avoid snooping during group work. You need to find a careful balance between showing interest in what a group is doing and appearing to snoop to be certain that the group is on task. In general the best strategy is to walk through the group to indicate an interest and to be ready if someone has a particular question.

Provide a choice during workshop activities. When suggesting activities and exercises, allow participants to choose among options for completing the task. As you're suggesting the activity, build in some strategies that participants can use to alter the activity to suit their needs. Some teachers may be shy or embarrassed about doing particular participatory activities; always leave the option open for people to observe others instead of doing the activity. Some will learn from this, and others will develop the confidence they need to try the next activity themselves.

Be enthusiastic about what you are presenting. Enthusiasm spreads. Share your excitement about the workshop topic so that the teachers can catch it, too.

Maintain interest in the workshop through various types of activities. Participants need to do different activities, and facilitators need to share using different techniques to motivate teachers. My most outrageous prop is the set of antlers I use with the book *Imogene's Antlers* by David Small: I put them on my head to tell the story. An unusual approach is especially effective if it is a departure from your usual style. Motivate with variety!

Selecting the Appropriate Interactive Strategy

It is your task as facilitator to select the one instructional strategy from among many that is most effective at a given point in the workshop. The National Staff Development Council suggests that a workshop facilitator consider the following when selecting an instructional strategy:

- Is knowledge, skill, or attitudinal learning involved?
- Is the strategy appropriate for the type of learning desired?
- Does the strategy lead to the desired learning in the simplest way possible?
- Do the participants have appropriate background knowledge, skills, or attitudes for the strategy?
- How much time does the strategy take?
- What are the space requirements?
- Are there any special materials required, and are they available?
- Are you, the facilitator, comfortable with the strategy?
- Are the participants comfortable with this type of strategy?
- Does the strategy require the participants' active or passive behavior? Is that type of behavior appropriate at this particular point of the workshop?

Choose the interactive strategy or strategies that seem best suited to your workshop, but do not overuse them in a single session. Too much group work can become a problem. I have heard teachers complain about the continual "sharing of ignorance," a feeling that is precipitated by too much group interaction. Make certain the strategies are relevant to the topic and are not perceived as a way to get the participants to do all the work.

Identify an interactive strategy you enjoyed in a workshop you recently attended. Then describe an interactive strategy you didn't like. Write down the specifics of each strategy, including the facilitator's introduction of the strategy, explanation of the strategy, and what participants did. Analyze why you enjoyed one strategy and not the other. Use this personal analysis to evaluate and select the interactive strategies for your workshop.

Be flexible in the timing of these interactive strategies. Give the participants enough time to complete the task and for adequate discussion but not so much time that the groups digress to unrelated topics. State an approximate length of time for the activity, and then watch to see how the teachers are doing. I generally circulate to answer any questions that might come up, as well as to determine how much time the groups will need to complete the particular task. If the groups are still on task but need more time than originally allotted, extend the time. If, however, the teachers are moving on to other topics, it is obvious that they have had enough time. Give them at least a thirty-second warning to wrap up their discussion.

Interactive Strategies for Workshops

For many teachers, being able to get up, move around, and talk with other teachers is important in a workshop. Interactive strategies help teachers become actively involved and provide an appropriate structure in which they can share their experiences. A number of interactive strategies that have been successful in teacher workshops are described below.

It's True Because I Said So

Robert Pike (1989) believes what my experience has validated: if the participants say for themselves that something is true, they will be inclined to believe it more than if someone else says it is true. Use an interactive strategy to involve the teachers in the planning as well as the implementation of the workshop. Ask the teachers to list topics related to the workshop subject; for example, what makes a good reading program. Most likely, they will list all of the factors you had previously identified in your planning stage, but you can fill in anything omitted. The teachers will have little difficulty accepting these topics because they're the ones who identified them.

Caution! If you use this technique, you need to be willing to accept the topics the participants suggest. If you are uncomfortable with this open-ended approach, choose a different strategy.

To Do Lists

Throughout the workshop, participants keep a list of ideas, concepts, techniques, and information that they identify as immediately applicable for them. Give the teachers short segments of time during the session to elaborate on precisely how they will use an idea described or alluded to in the workshop. Volunteers can exchange ideas at various times throughout the workshop. Other teachers may give a workshop idea new consideration after hearing one of their colleagues elaborate on its possible applicability. To further encourage action, ask the participants to identify a specific time within the next two months when they expect to be able to use the particular strategy or apply certain information.

I Believe in the Idea: I'll Use It

In this strategy, the participants analyze an idea from the workshop that seems to have merit and tell why they will use it in their classrooms. They also describe how the activity or information they have named is compatible with their overall teaching philosophy.

Thumbs Up

An effective yet quick and easy way to invite participation is to request that everyone respond to an idea, suggestion, or question by giving thumb signs or pencil signals. Physically representing their thoughts in this way focuses participants' attention on the task at hand.

Group Questions

Only the bravest teachers will ask a question in front of the total group. As an alternative, ask them to generate questions in smaller groups. Each group reviews the workshop content and develops two or three questions they would like to ask. While group members identify questions, they will also answer several preliminary questions. The final, unanswered questions are generally those of interest to everyone.

Three-Minute Activities

Also called "think, pair, and share," this strategy encourages participants to think about an idea, find a partner, and then trade insights. Rather than asking everyone in the group to share with everyone else, ask participants to discuss the idea with a small group or with a partner for three minutes. This speeds up the activity and gives reserved participants a more limited audience.

Carousel Brainstorming

Several small groups can brainstorm at once through carousel brainstorming, an idea developed by Pam Robbins. Divide participants into groups of about five people. Each group brainstorms and writes possibilities for the topic or question written on top of their sheet of newsprint. After approximately two minutes, the groups move to a different piece of newsprint and brainstorm possibilities for the topic or question listed on that sheet. They first read what the previous group has written and then add their new ideas. This continues until groups have brainstormed approximately six different topics. Participants then circulate and read what the various groups have had to say on the topics during a "gallery walk."

Jigsaw

One cooperative learning activity asks participants to become experts in a particular area and then share their newfound knowledge. There are various ways to organize the jigsaw activity, but the central concept is that groups of people are assigned or select topics that they teach to the others in the workshop. The groups decide collectively and cooperatively how they are going to share what they know. This activity draws on the experience the teachers bring to the workshop and acknowledges and reinforces mutual responsibility for learning.

Oprah Technique

If a group is large, it is difficult for others to hear when one of the participants is speaking. Do what Oprah Winfrey does on her show: give the microphone to the person who is talking. When the participant has the microphone, you won't need to repeat the information in order for everyone to hear, and you reinforce the idea that important information comes from everyone, not just the workshop facilitator.

Have I Got a Solution for You

Ask each of the teachers to think of a problem they are having that is related to the topic of the workshop. They write their problem on a card and initial the bottom. At various times during the workshop, participants select a card and write possible solutions to the problems. In a shorter workshop, have a particular time during which participants pass the cards, read the problems, and propose solutions. In longer workshops, participants may come in after a break, randomly select a problem card from a basket, write a solution, and then return the card to the basket. At the end of the workshop, participants retrieve their problem cards—with solutions, some of which are probably based on workshop content.

Key Word Mnemonics

As a technique to focus on the content of the workshop or to summarize information shared thus far, select a key word that is related to the workshop content. Participants then identify a word for each letter in the key word that is related to the important concepts of the workshop.

An acronym I use for a workshop regarding how to teach reading with literature, READERS, sums up the main components of the workshop. It can be used as an introduction to the main topics or as a summary.

R esources
E nthusiasm
A ssessment
D aily reading
E mpowerment
R esponse to reading
S kill/strategy development

Add-a-Caption

Project a transparency of a picture with no caption. Participants then write an appropriate caption connected to the workshop content. Look in the newspaper for wonderful photos to use for this activity. One of my personal favorites shows two young children, sound asleep in their strollers, looking very content and comfortable. Some possibilities for fitting captions include: "Lunch was great!" and "Break time!"

"I Want to Be Like . . ."

Finding out whom teachers esteem in their profession can tell a lot about their personal beliefs. Ask participants to describe the teacher they most admire and to give an example of the teacher's behavior to explain their admiration. Have them share this description with a partner, who must interpret the information and explain why the one teacher finds the other exemplary. Of course, there may be disagreements with the assessment, but it makes for an interesting discussion. Adapt this same technique for different topic areas as appropriate to the workshop content.

Icebreakers

Icebreakers or warm-ups are activities that get people moving and interacting with one another. They introduce participants to each other and to the topic of the workshop. Use icebreakers at the beginning of the workshop to get participants comfortable with one another and as energizers when concentration appears to be lagging. Because participants usually interact with many different people in a limited amount of time, icebreakers often promote team spirit. Though they tend to be fun, these icebreakers should be related to the content of the workshop, appropriate for your participants, and reasonable in number. In short workshops of less than one day, these types of activities should probably take up no more than fifteen minutes. Some people may not enjoy warm-ups, so don't insist upon participation.

Participant Scavenger Hunt

Teachers can learn more about one another through a participant scavenger hunt. Give participants a list of characteristics. Their task is to find others in the group for whom the various statements are true. You might, for example, ask them to find an only child, a parent of more than three children, a teacher who has worked for more than twenty-five years, a driver of a minivan, someone who has visited more than three foreign countries, and a teacher who has taught at least five grade levels or subjects. In order to foster further discussion, teachers can identify their characteristics, and these characteristic groups can be used later in the workshop.

An interesting adaptation of this activity is to ask participants to mark those items they think will be most difficult to find among the group. After the hunt is complete, ask for a show of hands of the people for whom each statement is true. Were the characteristics the people predicted to be hardest to find actually the ones that proved to be true least often?

What's in the Purse or Wallet

Before the workshop begins, ask volunteers to go through the contents of their purses or wallets to find five to ten items they are willing to show to other people. There are no specific requirements for the items other than that they be in the purse or wallet and that the person be willing to share them. Put the materials into envelopes with some type of owner identification. When the workshop begins, give one of these envelopes to each small group of participants. The groups examine the contents and draw conclusions about the owner of the materials regarding his or her personality, physical features, activities, and special characteristics. They share their conclusions with other groups who can challenge any inferences they hear that they do not think are supported by the facts the items represent. The owner then retrieves the materials and has an opportunity to respond to the conclusions drawn.

An alternative to this activity is to ask participants to go through their pocketbooks and wallets to find items that are significant for them, then explain this meaning to others.

Symbolically Speaking

Ask the teachers to draw symbols for their lives on their name tags or name plates. Have them explain their symbols to others in the group.

Let Me Introduce Myself

Participants take a piece of paper and use it to introduce themselves. Demonstrate this strategy first so that people will not simply write an introduction. For instance, I might take a piece of paper and scrunch it so that it resembles a microphone. I then introduce myself as someone who does a lot of public speaking. Someone once suggested that my paper looked like a tack, which is sharp, and the connection was clear.

Teachers will be very creative in this activity. It also gives them a prop to hide behind as they are becoming more comfortable with new people.

Advertise Yourself

Have participants write a short ad about themselves, featuring some unique trait or a skill of which they are especially proud. Collect and redistribute these ads and let participants identify each ad writer.

A similar strategy involves headlines. Participants write headlines about themselves, which are put on display. Other participants then try to identify the person each headline is describing.

Uniquely You

Challenge the participants to think of something that is true for them that they do not think is true for anyone else in the workshop. Encourage them to think of a personal experience they don't think anyone else has had. One of the most unusual experiences I've heard was from the teacher who admitted that she once got her head caught in a ditto machine. She was right—no one else in the group (perhaps even in the whole world) had had that experience. These unique features or personal experiences can either be announced to the group voluntarily or written on cards. Cards are then distributed randomly, and the participants try to find the person belonging to each card.

Tabloid Headlines

Have teachers write a tabloid headline that describes an experience they've had in their classrooms. Encourage them to work with a partner and come up with a headline for an actual event. For instance, "Aliens Invade School Library" would describe a display of new fantasy books; "Student Tells Wild Story About Visitors from Underground" would refer to a student's attempt to rid the schoolyard of moles; "One Rabbit Escapes: Ten Rabbits Found" would sum up how a school pet ran away, found a mate, and returned with babies. Share these headlines so that others can learn about their colleagues' school experiences.

Geographically Speaking

Judy Olson (Clair, Hoffman, and Olson, 1990) uses a technique that capitalizes on the mobility of our population as a way for people to find out about one another. An adaptation of her idea is to project a map of the United States using the overhead projector, and tell the participants to visualize the room as that map. They are to go to the approximate location of the city where they were born and introduce themselves to someone who is standing nearby. They then move to the city where they went to college and share with someone next to them a significant event from their time in college. They then move to the city where they got their first teaching job and describe the position to someone else nearby. Do a quick summary of the locations in which people lived for these major life events.

I Am Like a . . .

Have available an interesting collection of props such as an eggbeater, a book, a timer, and a pillow. Participants name one of the props and say why they are like that prop. This can also be used as a strategy for dividing people into groups—all the eggbeaters are in one group, all the timers in another, and so on.

A similar strategy involves titles of books, types of eggs, and other categories. Participants decide which of the suggested book titles could be the story of their life or whether they are most like an egg that is over-easy, hard-boiled, or scrambled.

"Sole" Mates

Give the participants a piece of paper cut in the shape of the bottom of a shoe. On various parts of the sole, each participant writes the same three professional characteristics: on the toe, the grade and subject they teach; on the arch or instep, the number of years they've been teaching; and on the heel, the year they started teaching. Their task, then, is to find other "sole mates" among the participants—people who have written the same information on the same shoe parts.

People Bingo

In a standard bingo card format, write twenty-five characteristics, one for each square, that participants are to find among the other teachers in the workshop. It's best to have a combination of professional and personal attributes on the card to invite socializing. When participants find someone with the attribute mentioned in the square, that person signs the card. Give participants a limited amount of time (approximately ten minutes) to reach bingo. The only rule is that no one can sign the same card for more than one attribute (i.e., no one can sign someone else's card more than once). See the Appendix for one example of a people bingo card.

We've Got You Covered

Find several books that relate to the topic of the workshop. Copy the covers of the books—in color, if possible. For greater durability, dry mount and laminate the covers onto cardboard. Cut these covers into thirds or fourths. Distribute one piece of a cover to each teacher, who then finds the others who have the rest of the puzzle. Together, the teachers write a synopsis of their book. This is also a good technique for introducing some of the major book resources in the topic area of your workshop.

Perfect Class

Participants are told that in their class there will be three students of their choice next year. These three students can be of any age and can be fictional or real, alive or dead. Teachers decide whom they would like to have as their special students and why. Teachers may decide individually on their students and then discuss their decision with two or three other teachers. Share some of the student selections with the entire group.

Instant Fun

This is for the group that really needs to get going. Pass out sheets with the following instructions:

- All blue-eyed people stand and twirl.
- Everybody who is over 5' 8" shout "King Kong!"
- All people who wear a size 6 shoe, clap your hands 6 times.
- If you are wearing anything red, you have a particular job. Tell the teacher on your right that you do not now like and have never in the past liked the way he or she parts his or her hair.
- If you have gum with you, smack loudly twice.
- If your sister is married, remember it is nobody's business. Tell the person on your left that you feel this way.
- If you use cream in your coffee, get up and look under your chair.
- If you have ever smoked a cigar, shout "I deny it!"
- If you have brown eyes, bow to the audience.
- If you use the hunt-and-peck typing system, practice on your table.
- All who have freckles run around the table to your right three times.
- If you have an "e" and an "a" in your name, say "e, ah."
- If you are married, make a circle in the air with your arm.
- If you know how to ride a bike, demonstrate. Go around the table to the left.
- If somebody forced you to come today, hit your fist on the table and shout "I resent this action!"
- If you had a good breakfast, stand up and pat your stomach.
- If you can't roller-skate, try it.
- If you can swim, show us. Swim three strokes to the left, then get the water out of your ear.
- If you have ever driven a truck, call out "Honk! Honk!"
- Hop once for each of your children.
- If you have ever seen a bear, growl.
- If you've ever been chicken, squawk.
- If you are finished, pound the table three times, throw this paper on the floor, and stomp on it.

Room Arrangements for Involvement

The physical arrangement of the workshop facility may indicate to the teachers how much participation will be expected or encouraged. This does not mean that you cannot encourage participation in any type of facility, but there are certain ways to set up a room that can indicate the type of participation expected.

Figure 8.1 shows the chairs are arranged in a semicircular shape rather than in straight rows for easier viewing. A little space between chairs makes participants more comfortable. This indicates a formal, listening-only type of workshop.

Often referred to as classroom style, the arrangement in Figure 8.2 gives participants a place to write. For longer periods of time, it is essential that people have somewhere to lean; otherwise, fatigue tends to set in. The tables make small group discussions easier.

The seating arrangement illustrated in Figure 8.3 gives participants a feeling of being in a smaller group, as the subgroups are physically obvious. Position the chairs around approximately two-thirds of the table so that the view of the

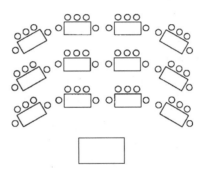

Figure 8.2 *Large group workshop: Participants seated at tables in a semicircle*

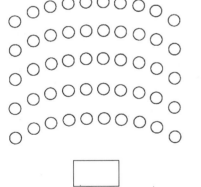

Figure 8.1 *Large group workshop: Participants seated in chairs in rows*

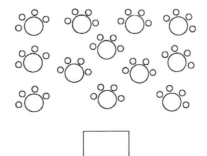

Figure 8.3 *Large group workshop: Participants seated at round tables*

front is unencumbered. This position indicates that the workshop will be highly participative and the facilitator really a resource and a catalyst.

In Conclusion

Teachers indicate that their involvement and participation in a workshop is essential for its success. While too much involvement and interaction can become tedious, it is important that teachers in the workshop have an opportunity to talk and work with one another. By selecting from and adapting the involvement and interactive strategies described in this chapter, you can increase teacher participation without increasing anxiety.

Works Cited and Suggested Readings

Boyle, Patrick G. *Planning Better Programs.* Chapter 16. New York: McGraw-Hill, 1981

Brookfield, Stephen. *The Skillful Teacher.* Chapters 8 and 9. San Francisco: Jossey-Bass, 1990

Clair, Joan; Hoffman, Connie; and Olson, Judy. *Getting It Started, Keeping It Going, Wrapping It Up.* Federal Way, WA: VISTA Associates, 1990

Davis, Larry Nolan. *Planning, Conducting, and Evaluating Workshops.* Austin, TX: Learning Concepts, 1974

Kahler, Alan A., et al. *Methods in Adult Education.* Chapter 6. Danville, IL: Interstate, 1985

Knox, Alan B. *Helping Adults Learn.* Chapters 7 and 8. San Francisco: Jossey-Bass, 1987

Moffett, Cerylle; and Warger, Cynthia. *The Human Resource Development Program Handbook: A Practical Guide for Staff Developers.* Part 2. Alexandria, VA: Association for Supervision and Curriculum Development, 1988

Pike, Robert W. *Creative Training Techniques Handbook.* Chapter 5. Minneapolis, MN: Lakewood Books,1989

Powers, Bob. *Instructor Excellence: Mastering the Delivery of Training.* Chapters 6 and 9. San Francisco: Jossey-Bass, 1992

SET

Honor your audience with anxiety.
—Madeleine L'Engle

After you have planned the workshop and before you are ready to begin, turn your attention to a few additional details: you should make sure the visuals for the workshop are prepared and the workshop facility is ready for use, with all materials and equipment set up. Most importantly, *you* need to be ready, so that you know that you and the participants are going to enjoy and learn from your workshop.

★ ★ ★

9

Visuals in the Workshop

We live in a visual society. It is only natural that teachers will expect visuals in a workshop. Because of our collective experience with television and advertising, we have become accustomed to seeing visuals of a certain quality that present information in a pleasing yet effective manner. Directions given orally are much more difficult to understand than directions that can be seen and read.

How Visuals Can Help

People use visuals to enhance their understanding every day. It is not only logical but imperative that you begin from the teachers' experience and include visuals in your workshop. Effective visuals can help convey your message in the workshop for a number of reasons.

Visuals enhance the point you're making. It seems that people put more emphasis on what they see rather than what they hear. When a facilitator speaks about three points, people may listen politely. If a visual shows these same three points, however, chances are that participants will write those points down. This is the very reason you use the chalkboard in your classroom—when you write something down, the students pay particular attention.

Think about the visuals that were part of a workshop you attended. Make a list of those that you specifically remember. Write a brief description of each visual listed and why it made a particular impression on you. This information will help you decide when to use a visual to increase its impact.

Visuals increase the potential to reach more learners. Some learners have a strong visual modality, and when they see something in conjunction with a new concept or idea, they understand it better than if they just hear it (Guild and Garger, 1985). Use of visuals, then, can better accommodate these visual learners.

Visuals attract and maintain participants' attention. People are used to visual stimulation. A well-produced or provocative visual can help participants focus on the point being discussed. Because teachers are accustomed to visuals, if you omit visuals from your workshop, you risk losing participants' attention.

Visuals can add realism to the workshop. Visuals can help provide common scenarios for the participants to consider. While it is not often possible to bring the students to the workshop, it is easy to bring visuals that show or are made by the students.

A simple exercise helps to show the importance of visual material for increased understanding. You will need a blank sheet of paper and a pencil.

1. Place the paper lengthwise on a flat surface.
2. At the bottom of the sheet, draw two small squares approximately 3″ apart.
3. Inside each square, across the bottom, draw a series of half circles.
4. Draw a large rectangle on top of and connecting both squares.
5. On top of the upper right corner of the rectangle, draw a circle with a diameter that is the same as the height of the rectangle.
6. Imagine the circle as the face of a clock. Draw a large "S" starting at the five o'clock position in the circle and extending outside the circle.
7. Draw another "S" parallel to it, approximately 1/8″ from the first.
8. Draw another circle in the upper left corner of the first circle that is half inside of the first circle and half outside of it.
9. In the upper left corner of the rectangle, draw another "S."
10. Just above the two parallel "S's," draw two ovals, the inner one in the lower half of the outer one.
11. As you can see, you have just drawn a stylized elephant.

After you have followed the directions, read them to someone else so they can complete the drawing based on what they hear. Read only what is written and give no additional explanation.

Compare the two drawings. When you read the directions, you can review them for clarification. Someone listening to the directions, however, must interpret them without any visual help. This is a clear reminder of the difficulty workshop participants have when they only hear concepts; the addition of visuals increases the likelihood that the teachers will understand what is presented.

Visuals help to illustrate factors that are difficult to picture in the mind's eye. When you present information that is new to the participants, you may have to let them see it to make them believe it. Visuals showing how teachers and students are implementing the ideas you suggest help participants imagine how the concept can be put into practice.

Visuals decrease the likelihood of misunderstanding. If participants can see as well as hear the point being made, there is less chance of misunderstanding. There are many words, for example, that sound the same but have different meanings. Visuals can provide the necessary context for these words. Without visual cues, a spoken *right/write* could mean to correct, or to put a pen to paper, or it could be a directional term. A visual makes the meaning very clear.

Visuals help to organize the presentation. By arranging the visuals in sequence, you can use overhead transparencies, for example, instead of note cards to remember what is coming next. Further, visuals can help assure that you don't forget an important point that you wanted to make; if you have a picture relating to an idea, you'll either remember to mention it or consciously decide to omit it.

Visuals can provide a confidence shield between the facilitator and the participants. New facilitators are sometimes overly nervous about being in front of their peers. Visual aids can bolster your confidence by providing something for the participants to look at other than you and, as we've seen, by alleviating any worries you might have about forgetting the topic organization.

Visuals are used to support, not replace, the facilitator. While the visuals are meant to help convey the message, it is the interaction between the facilitator and the participants that makes the difference between an effective and an ineffective workshop. Use visuals only when they enhance your ideas by defining or identifying, clarifying, proving, or strengthening a point or generating a mood.

Designing the Visuals for the Workshop

Workshop participants will generally decide whether to pay attention to a visual or to ignore it during the first ten seconds it is shown. In this age of advanced technology and sophisticated viewers, it is more important than ever that the visuals used in workshops are of sufficiently high quality to please the sensibilities of the participants. Although the teachers won't expect Disney, they will expect some well-thought-out and nicely produced visuals in your presentation.

Basic Design Principles for Visuals

Because of the familiarity your participants have with visuals, you should apply some basic design principles to compound the impact your visuals will have.

Keep the visual simple. Confine each visual to a single idea. Rather than listing four points on a single slide or overhead transparency, put each point on a separate image with an appropriate illustration. The transparency in Figure 9.1 has too much visual information. It is better to make a separate transparency for each concept as shown in Figure 9.2.

Keep the visual organized. The arrangement of the information should enhance the message. Sequence the elements of the visual so that the participants know how to view it and in which direction to read. For clarity, the information should read from left to right or from top to bottom (see Figure 9.3).

For two weeks save the promotions and advertisements you receive in the mail at home and at school. Without regard for the content, evaluate the materials as to their visual appeal. Separate the materials into stacks of those that appeal to you and those that are of little visual interest. List specific characteristics of the materials that caught your attention. Reevaluate the materials that did not capture your initial interest. Are they lacking in certain visual characteristics? Remember these visually appealing aspects as you design the materials.

Leave ample white or open space on the visual. Open space helps the eye to focus on the important information, as in Figure 9.4.

Divide space on the visual in an interesting manner. It isn't necessary to focus on the center of the visual; sometimes the focus can be in the left corner or upper middle instead (see Figure 9.5). Use text and graphics to make the focal point of the visual obvious.

Balance the visual information so that it is stable and pleasing to the eye. Make a path for the eye to follow, but place the information so that the visual doesn't look lopsided. Figure 9.6 shows how you can compensate for fewer words in a particular part of the visual.

To highlight part of a visual, make it different from the rest. Use underlining, italic, bold type, or outline letters to focus attention on a particular idea (see Figure 9.7). Make headline or main points larger or bolder than subheads to add emphasis.

Consider putting a headline on each visual. A headline helps the participants focus on the main idea of the visual. As in Figure 9.8, a headline should contain a noun and a verb that capture the key point.

Purposes of Literature

Enjoying a good story

Stimulating the imagination; encouraging a sense of wonder

Understanding ourselves and others

Exploring the nature of language
- **dialects**
- **sounds**
- **qualities of words**

Learning of other times and places

Seeking new information

Figure 9.1 *Too much information*

Purposes of Literature

Seeking New Information

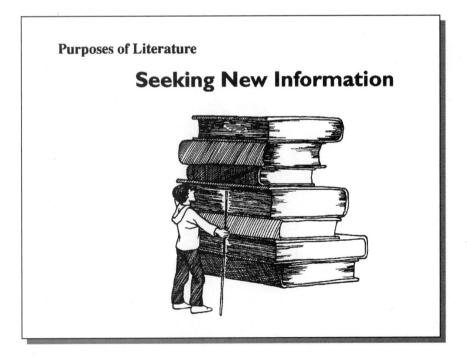

Figure 9.2 *Single concept*

Return the Author to Reading

- **Reading is an interactive process.**
- **Good readers think about the author's intent.**
- **Good readers seek out specific authors.**
- **Reading comprehension improves when readers are encouraged to think about the author.**

Figure 9.3 *Clear organization*

When's Lunch?

Figure 9.4 *Open space on a visual*

Figure 9.5 *Interesting spatial arrangement*

Keep items in lists grammatically and visually parallel. Consistently begin a line with a capital or lowercase letter, the same spacing, and the same part of speech (see Figure 9.9).

Check carefully for errors. A small error on the visual will be magnified many times when it is projected. Check, recheck, and get someone else to check spelling, grammar, punctuation, and correctness of numbers. Use a spelling checker on your computer-generated visuals, but remember that although it will tell you if a word is misspelled, it will not tell you if you have used the correct word.

Put the most important parts of the visual at the top. Participants in the back of the room need to see everything, and heads will block the view of what is on the bottom of the visual. Figure 9.10 is an example of an appropriately top-heavy layout.

Thinking About Text
Although many visuals contain words, they are intended to be used in a workshop and should require the facilitator's explanation. The transparency master pictured in Figure 9.11 is a good example of a workshop visual, as its message is unclear without the explanation from the facilitator.

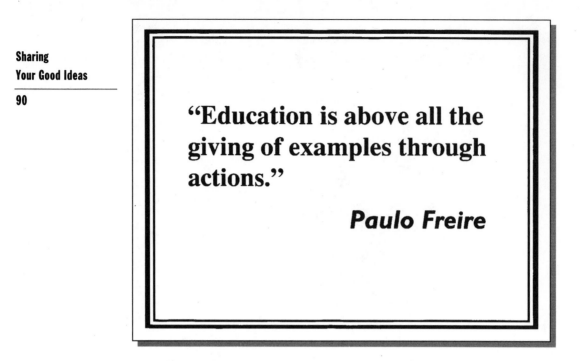

Figure 9.6 *Balance*

Figure 9.7 *Change of type*

To help you plan your text, write a paragraph explaining the information you want to present in your visual. Then rewrite the paragraph, eliminating descriptive and connecting words. The final version of your text will more than likely be a list that makes little sense on its own.

The general rule for visuals is the less text the better. A general rule that some use is no more than six lines, and no more than six words per line. Think of yourself as a headline writer when you write text for a visual.

There are some additional techniques to help you decide what text to include on a visual in order to increase its impact:

- Write the message with a marker on 8 1/2″ x 11″ paper. If it looks as though there are too many words, try at least two visuals for that amount of information.
- Put text on the visual in the order you want to talk about it.
- Omit anything you do not plan to talk about.
- Don't overload the visual with numbers; include only those that are important for participants to remember. Shock-value numbers don't belong on the visual.

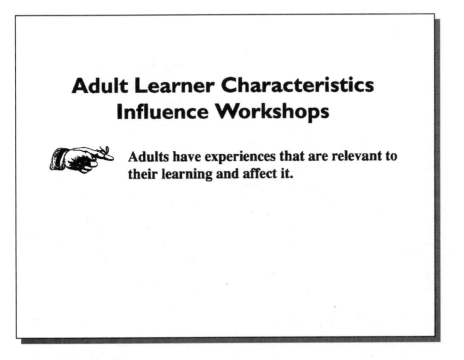

Figure 9.8 *Headlines*

Type

After you have determined what you want to say on the visual, you need to identify the kind of lettering that will best convey your message. You probably haven't given much thought to lettering; it is easy to ignore unless it is disruptive.

You can identify the importance of the typeface style when you see the same word printed in various sizes and styles of type:

happiness happiness happiness **happiness** *happiness* **happiness**

anger anger anger **anger** *anger* **anger**

humor humor humor **humor** *humor* **humor**

sadness sadness sadness **sadness** *sadness* **sadness**

happiness happiness happiness happiness

anger anger anger

Be certain that the type style and size you use reflects the feeling of the message.

While you want to gain your participants' attention, you also want them to be able to read the visual. Below are some guidelines that can help you decide on the appropriate combination of typeface and type size for your visual.

Use an easy-to-read typeface. Here are a couple of examples: **Helvetica is an effective sans-serif typeface.** Times, which this book is set in, is an effective serif typeface.

Glance through the typefaces in the books you use with your students and that appear in materials you receive in the mail. Identify any differences in type or lettering in the two kinds of materials. As you evaluate the two, you will see that certain typefaces make an impact whereas others increase the readability of the text.

Use both upper- and lowercase. ALTHOUGH YOU MAY THINK THAT ALL CAPITAL LETTERS PROVIDE GREATER IMPACT, THEY ARE IN FACT MORE DIFFICULT TO READ than a mix of uppercase and lowercase letters. Readers read faster when they read what they normally see in print.

Avoid the use of hyphens on visuals. They are dis-

Preparing a Workshop

1. Identify the subject.

2. Analyze the participants.

3. Gather necessary data.

4. Identify the critical attribute.

5. Identify workshop goals and aims.

6. Identify influencing and interactive strategies.

7. Plan a presentation sequence.

8. Prepare materials and outline.

9. Evaluate the workshop.

Figure 9.9 *Using verbs*

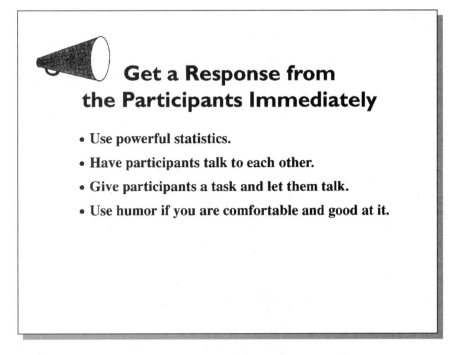

Get a Response from the Participants Immediately

- Use powerful statistics.
- Have participants talk to each other.
- Give participants a task and let them talk.
- Use humor if you are comfortable and good at it.

Figure 9.10 *Placement of important information*

ruptive and require the reader to rethink what is printed (see Figure 9.12).

Italic print on visuals is more difficult to read and does not provide emphasis. If Figure 9.13 were projected onto a screen, viewers would have difficulty differentiating the italics from the roman type; at a distance, viewers can better distinguish underlining. Underlining also helps viewers to focus on the text.

Limit the number of typefaces that you use on all visuals in your workshop. A limited number provides consistency. Too many typefaces can be confusing and make the visual look cluttered. Compare Figure 9.14 and Figure 9.15; which is easier to read?

Use no more than three type sizes in a single visual. The larger type sizes are good for emphasis, but too many changes in size can make the eye tired.

Bold type is easier to read in visuals. Use bold type whenever possible on visuals, as the letters are wider, darker, and easier to see. The difference is clear in the visuals pictured in Figures 9.16 and 9.17.

Use bullets when itemizing points of equal importance. Bullets give the eye an indication that there is a listing but that no single point is more important than another (see Figure 9.18).

Use numbers when indicating importance or chronological order. Numbers indicate a hierarchy and are effective in showing items that belong in an order, as illustrated in Figure 9.19.

Figure 9.11 *Facilitator's explanation needed*

The library media specialist's role in literature-based instruction

Publicize your knowledge about what's good, new, and rele‐ vant in children's literature.

Figure 9.12 *Avoid hyphenated words*

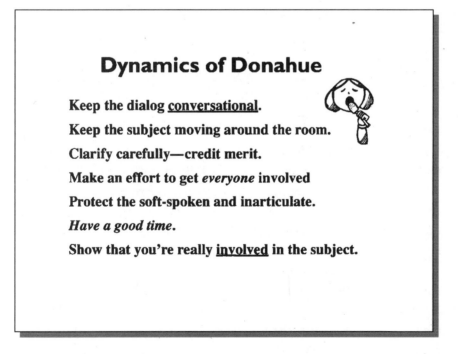

Dynamics of Donahue

Keep the dialog <u>conversational</u>.

Keep the subject moving around the room.

Clarify carefully—credit merit.

Make an effort to get *everyone* involved

Protect the soft-spoken and inarticulate.

Have a good time.

Show that you're really <u>involved</u> in the subject.

Figure 9.13 *Avoid italics*

Study the figure below to determine whether it seems to be an example of an effective visual to use in a workshop based upon the design principles just described. Identify which parts of the visual could be improved. Identify any design techniques that were incorporated into this visual that would be appropriate for all of your workshop visuals.

A Literature-Based Reading Program

- **Uses whole-text experiences.**
- **Uses books with natural, uncontrolled language.**
- **Includes time for reading aloud to students.**
- **Includes time for students to read silently.**
- **Allows for student selection of reading materials.**
- **Incorporates skills instruction in a meaningful context.**
- **Stresses writing and other output activities.**

Adding Color

Used appropriately, color can enhance visuals by adding variety and impact. One, two, or three colors have a significant effect, but more than that can cause confusion. Use color to organize and sequence information—contrasting colors to illustrate contrasting concepts or to suggest a major change, and shades of the same color to suggest minor change. Add color either when you first create the visual or while you are showing the visual during the workshop.

As you design your visuals, consider the particular characteristics of certain colors (Raines, 1989). Blue, for example, is the least permanent of the colors; it fades most quickly and is most susceptible to temperature variations. Red is the most difficult color to see from a distance. Yellow is ineffective as a background color. When you pick a color, be certain its characteristics are appropriate for the medium.

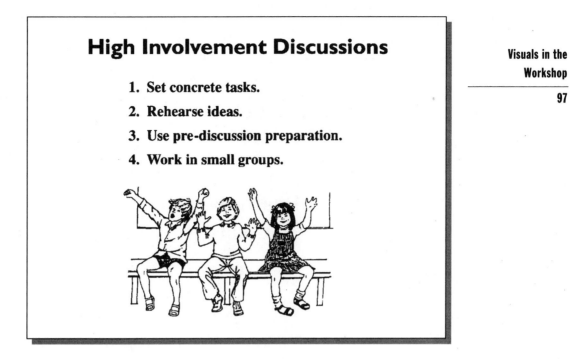

Figure 9.14 *A single typeface*

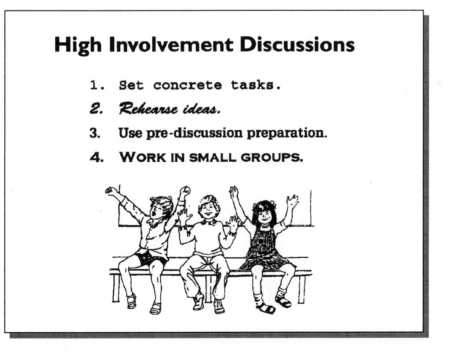

Figure 9.15 *Too many typefaces*

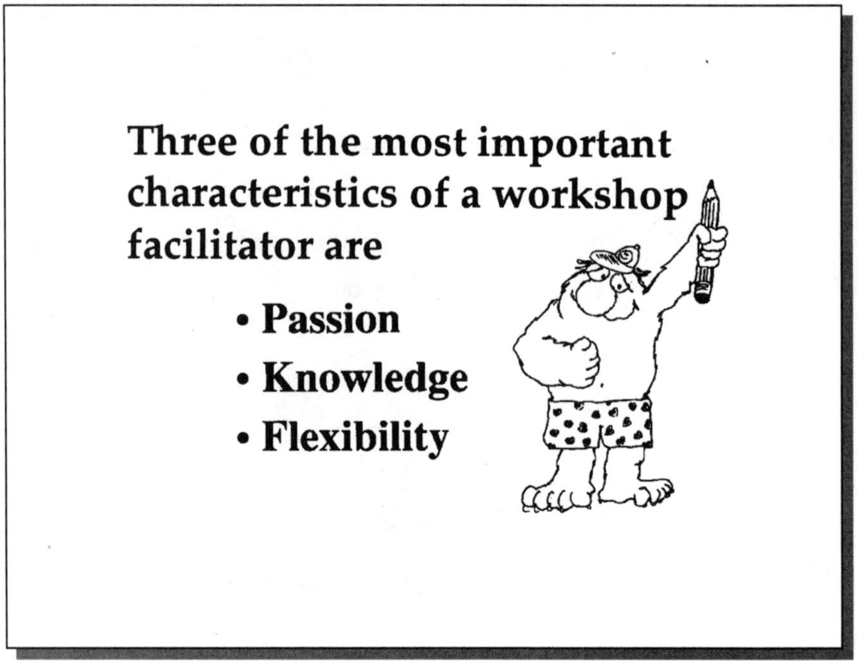

> # Three of the most important characteristics of a workshop facilitator are
>
> - **Passion**
> - **Knowledge**
> - **Flexibility**

Figure 9.16 *Bold typeface*

Graphics that Grab

Pictures can make a visual more memorable. Be certain that the graphics you use are copyright-free and add to rather than detract from the overall message of the visual. In the overhead transparency shown in Figure 9.20, the visual reinforces the message that an important reason for children to read is for their personal enjoyment.

Clip-art books are a good source of public-domain illustrations that are ready to use and professionally done. Some sources of clip art include: Dover Publications (180 Varick Street, New York, NY 10014) and REDI-ART (30 E. 10th Street, New York, NY 10002). Check the copyright page of each clip-art book for specific limitations and requirements of use, as many of the pictures may be reproduced for workshop visuals and packets but not for commercial publication.

Clip-art programs are also available for computers. An especially good series is Click Art by Phil Frank (T/Maker Co., 1390 Villa Street, Mountain View, CA 94041). Specific titles include *Color Graphics for Presentations, Events and Holiday Cartoons,* and *Holidays.* Another software package is 3G Graphics (11410 NE 124th, Suite 6155, Kirkland, WA 98034). Specific titles include *Accents & Borders, Business I,* and *Images with Impact.*

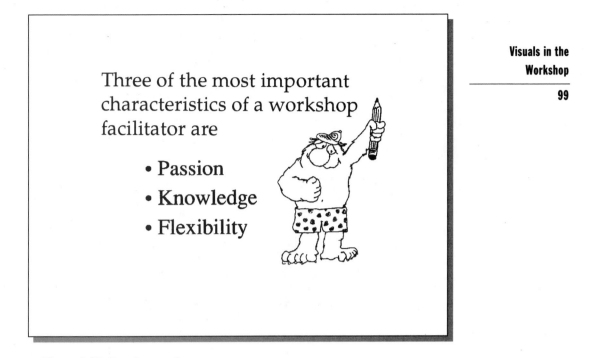

Figure 9.17 *Regular typeface*

You can also compile your own graphics file. Begin collecting noncopyrighted drawings (black-line drawings work best) that appear in community college catalogs, flyers, and Sunday papers. Posters that are placed on telephone poles may have useful images that can be cut out as well. When it's time to create a visual, look through your file to find just what you need. Some people arrange the graphics they collect by topic or subject. I prefer to go through all the graphics each time I need one, as different pictures inspire me in different ways at different times. Choose the system that works best for you.

Rubber stamps are an easy way to get professional-looking graphics, though the images may need to be copied and enlarged before you can use them on the visual. Rubber stamps can tie together your workshop handouts and materials as well.

You can have your own rubber stamp made if you prefer ready access to a graphic you intend to use and reuse; look in the yellow pages under "Rubber Stamps" for a source for producing your own graphic. A growing number of companies are creating ready-made rubber stamps. (See a list of companies and a sample of stamps at the end of this chapter.)

Identify the design principles and suggestions regarding text, type, and graphics that are exemplified in the visual below. Make a list of how the visual is effective and indicate specific elements that could be improved.

Purposes of Literature

Understanding Ourselves and Others

Looking Like a Pro with Visuals

The most professionally produced visuals can detract from a workshop if they are not used appropriately. You can follow a few guidelines to make the difference between visuals that enhance the workshop and visuals that get in the way.

Visuals need to be visible by everyone. Referring to something on the visual that only the people in the front can see is frustrating for those in the back. If a particular visual is small but important, move throughout the workshop so that everyone can see it, put it on display for later viewing, or change its format for easier viewing. Rather than holding up an open book and pointing out an illustration few participants can see, secure permission from the publisher to make the picture into a slide or transparency so that everyone can see it.

Give yourself plenty of time to plan, produce, and revise the visuals. Don't cheat the workshop participants because you procrastinated on preparations or still prefer the old way. For many visuals you should make at least one prototype before deciding on the final version.

Use the appropriate visual format for the activity or point you're trying to make. Each medium has distinct advantages and disadvantages. Consider these in conjunction with your goal and choose the medium that most effectively communicates your ideas. Read through the sections in Chapter 10 outlining the advantages and disadvantages of the different media.

Become familiar with the various media, and choose the medium for which you can produce the most professional-looking visual given your resources. Some visuals require special equipment and expertise. Video, for example, is excellent for showing classroom situations, but it can be very costly and time-consuming to produce a good videotape. Determine the type of visual you can produce with the best results.

Use only up-to-date visuals. Check the accuracy of numbers and facts presented. If the visual shows signs of extensive use, make a new one.

When requesting equipment for your workshop, be very specific. Request brand names to increase the likelihood that the audiovisual supplier will bring exactly what you need. Be very specific about the types of visuals you will be using with the equipment, so that the equipment matches your format.

Remove visuals from view or sight after you are finished talking about or using them. The participants will wonder why the visual is shown if it is not the object of discussion. They may be focusing on the reason for the visual rather than the content of the workshop. Only certain types of visuals should

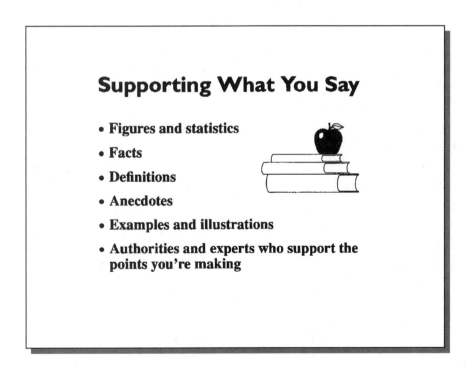

Figure 9.18 *Use of bullets*

Developing an Interdisciplinary Unit

1. Consult with other people involved.

2. Establish goals—long and short term.

3. Make sure objectives strengthen each discipline.

4. Web activities related to theme.

5. Identify skills needed in the "process."

6. Gather materials.

7. Teach unit.

8. Enrich and/or remediate.

9. Evaluate.

Figure 9.19 *Use of numbers*

be on view after they have been discussed, and these include an overview visual, posters, and examples that teachers might want to refer to during breaks.

When you turn on the projector, be certain that there is something to see. The participants will look toward the light when it is turned on and will be expecting to see a visual. Turn the projector off when there is no image to see.

Make sure the air vent on your projector is clear. A blocked air vent can cause the equipment to overheat, which could damage the visuals.

Face the group. Even during slide presentations, be certain that you are facing the participants so that everyone can hear. Your voice carries much better when you face the group, and your presence is reinforced.

When possible, set up the screen or flip chart at a 45° angle slightly to one side of the center of the room. Center stage belongs to the facilitator, not the screen. Prior to the workshop, be certain that the screen or flip chart is visible from all seats in the room.

Carry extra media materials with you so you will never be without. It is difficult to know what will be available at the workshop site, so carry what you need. Items to carry include: bulbs for projectors, extension cords, masking tape, overhead projector pens, remote, extension cord for the remote, and three-pronged adapters.

Prepare backup copies of all your visuals. Too often things are inadvertently damaged or lost. Always have a replacement ready.

Do not overload your workshop with too many visuals. Too many visuals will reduce their effectiveness. Remember that the visuals are for support and are not intended to replace the facilitator.

In Conclusion

Visuals are an integral part of your workshop or presentation. Not only do they help to convey information and appeal to various senses, but participants are accustomed to visual images and will expect them in the workshop. The suggestions presented in this chapter can help you plan both the development and the use of the visuals for the maximum benefit in your workshop.

Figure 9.20 *Graphics*

Contact these companies directly for complete catalogs.

All Night Media
PO Box 2666
San Anselmo, CA 94960

Graphistamp
Imprints Graphic Studio, Inc.
Carmel-by-the-Sea, CA 93921

Hero Art Rubber Stamps
1998 San Pablo Ave.
Berkeley, CA 94702

Kidstamps
PO Box 18699
Cleveland Heights, OH 44118

Personal Stamp Exchange
345 S. McDowell Blvd.
Suite 324
Petaluma, CA 94952

Rubber-Stampede
PO Box 246
Berkeley, CA 94701

Works Cited and Suggested Readings

Considine, David M.; and Haley, Gail E. *Visual Messages: Integrating Imagery into Instruction.* Chapters 1 and 2. Englewood, CO: Teacher Ideas Press, 1992

Guild, Pat B.; and Garger, Stephen. *Marching to Different Drummers.* Alexandria, VA: Association for Supervision and Curriculum Development, 1985

Heinich, R.; Molenda, M.; and Russell, J. *Instructional Media and the New Technologies of Instruction.* Chapters 1, 2, and 3. New York: Macmillan, 1993

Kemp, Jerrold E. *Planning and Producing Audio Visual Materials.* 5th ed. New York: Harper & Row, 1989

King, Kenneth L., et al. *A Systematic Approach to Instructional Media Competency: Orientation, Operation, Action.* 5th ed. Dubuque, IA: Kendall/Hunt, 1985

Locatis, Craig N.; and Atkinson, Francis D. *Media and Technology for Education and Training.* Chapters 4, 5, and 6. Columbus, OH: Merrill, 1984

Pike, Robert W. *Creative Training Techniques Handbook.* Chapter 4. Minneapolis, MN: Lakewood Books, 1989

Powers, Bob. *Instructor Excellence: Mastering the Delivery of Training.* Chapter 10. San Francisco: Jossey-Bass, 1992

Raines, Claire. *Visual Aids in Business.* Section 2. Los Altos, CA: Crisp, 1989

Simonson, Michael; and Volker, Roger. *Media Planning and Production.* Chapter 3. Columbus, OH: Merrill, 1984

Smith, Terry C. *Making Successful Presentations: A Self-Teaching Guide.* 2d ed. Chapter 5. New York: John Wiley & Sons, 1991

10

Visual Media Options

You can use any of several media to present visuals during a workshop; some you have probably already used with your students in the classroom. In this chapter suggestions and strategies for working with the four of the most popular and effective workshop media—overhead projections, slides, flip charts, and video—are described.

Overhead Projections

Overhead transparencies are some of the most popular and helpful visuals for workshops. The necessary equipment is readily available, and facilitators and participants alike are comfortable with the medium.

As you consider when and whether to use overhead projections for your workshop, keep in mind their advantages and disadvantages.

Advantages
- Overhead projections can be used with all group sizes as long as the room is arranged properly.
- The room lights stay on, so the participants can see the facilitator as well as the visual.
- The overhead projector is positioned in the front of the room, allowing the facilitator to face the participants.
- Overhead projectors are usually provided without cost to presenters at conferences and are generally on hand in schools.
- Overhead transparencies allow for flexibility in a workshop because they can be easily rearranged as the content and participants require.
- Overhead transparencies allow for interaction, as they can be written on while they are projected.
- Transparencies can be modified as additional information is shared during the workshop.
- Overhead transparencies are easy to transport because they are lightweight and fit wherever a piece of notebook-sized paper fits.

- There are many ways to produce overhead transparencies.
- With the availability of photocopiers and color copiers, high-quality trans-
parencies can be made quickly and relatively inexpensively.
- Transparencies can be easily updated and replaced.
- Participants can have paper copies of the masters used for the transpar-
encies shared in the workshop.

Disadvantages
- The fans on some of the older overhead projectors often make a distracting
hum.
- There is a tendency for the facilitator to become tied to the projector, as the
use of transparencies often requires significant facilitator narration.
- The quality of the projected image is dependent on the quality of the
machine and may be distorted.
- Room lighting conditions can affect the projected image, making it look
washed out.

Producing Effective Overhead Transparencies

Overhead transparencies are some of the easiest visuals to produce, yet they
are often poorly conceived and developed.

To create your overhead transparencies, I suggest the following guidelines.

Think of an overhead transparency you have seen used effectively in a workshop. Write all that you can remember about the visual. Think about how you can adapt the best aspects of this visual for the overhead transparencies you produce. Similarly, describe a transparency used in a workshop that was unsatisfactory. Use this description to remind you of the pitfalls of overhead transparency production.

The image should be no more than 7 1/2" x 9" for a standard-sized transparency. All parts of an image of this size will be clearly visible with no words or graphics running off the edge.

Complete the transparency test for each transparency you produce. Tape the typed copy of the transparency text to a wall. If you can't read it from a distance of 8 to 12 feet, it will not be legible to the participants. Letters on the original should be at least 30 points (1/4 inch) high for easy visibility.

Horizontal transparencies are generally easiest to read. The horizontal format allows for more text to be written across, which is more readable. There may be situations when the vertical format is necessary, however, as when the original graphic or chart is vertical and cannot be rotated because of size limitations.

The horizontal format in Figure 10.1 is easy to read and allows plenty of space for each response, allows less space after each statement and pushes the last statement down to the bottom of the screen. It is best to have all horizontal or all vertical transparencies in one workshop, so that they are all easily visible with no changes needed in screen position. After the screen is set up for one format, switching formats might mean that viewers in the front block others' sight lines.

Adding frames to transparencies makes them more durable and gives them a finished look. The frames fit the stage of the overhead projector so that no light is visible around the edge of the transparency. The frames are also a good space for noting important information you don't want to forget. Frames do add considerable weight to the transparencies, however.

Looking Like a Pro with Overhead Projections

Once you've decided to use overhead projections and have produced quality transparencies, you'll want to put the medium to its best use.

Arrive early and make certain that you know how to switch the projector on and off. Some projectors have switches and some have bars; be sure you know how to operate the one for your workshop.

Check to be certain that the overhead projector has an extra bulb and know how to access it. Most projectors now have two bulbs within the projector, and all you need to do is move a lever to get a new bulb and light.

Set up the projector in the most advantageous place. Put the projector where you will be seen by the most people and will not be in the way of the projected image. Be certain, too, that the projector itself is not obstructing anyone's view.

Put the screen up as high as possible. A large screen that goes to the floor is less useful than a smaller screen that is placed on risers. The information at the bottom of the screen is most difficult to see, so set the screen as high as possible off the floor.

If possible, tilt the top of the screen forward to prevent the "keystone" effect that makes transparencies difficult to see. The keystone is the trapezoidal image you sometimes see when an overhead transparency is projected. If you can't move the screen, you may want to change the projection angle of the projector by raising it.

Avoid having a light source shining on the screen. If the lights in the room cannot be turned off in banks, disconnect the light or lights that are making the image on the screen difficult to see. Also, be certain that light from windows is not interfering with the image on the screen.

Remember that transparencies are placed on the projector so that you can read from them. Place the transparency on the overhead projector so that you

Workshop Wisdoms

A true-false test regarding research about effective workshops

	True	False
1. The best time for workshops is at the beginning of the day.	_____	_____
2. The best place for a screen is directly behind the presenter.	_____	_____
3. Adults learn easily with nonhuman media.	_____	_____
4. "One-shot" sessions are highly effective.	_____	_____
5. Adults learn brand new concepts easily and quickly.	_____	_____
6. Adults are interested in new information for its own sake.	_____	_____
7. A good presenter can present anything.	_____	_____
8. Adults need limited directions for independent learning.	_____	_____
9. If adults are interested, they can listen for a long time.	_____	_____
10. Overheads are the most effective media for workshops.	_____	_____

Figure 10.1 *Horizontal format*

can stand next to the projector and read the transparency by looking at the overhead projector stage. If you can read the transparencies when standing next to the projector, the participants can read them, as well. There is no need to turn to the screen to determine whether the transparencies are positioned correctly.

Make cardboard frames of various widths that can be used with smaller transparencies. If your transparencies are smaller than the stage of the projector, a frame of light will appear around them when they are projected. Remedy this by placing a temporary cardboard frame of the appropriate width around the overhead projector stage, so that the light source is only as large as your transparency.

Arrange your transparencies in the order you plan to use them and place them near the projector. Be certain, too, to leave some space to put the transparencies after you are done with them; a box behind the projector works well. If you place them into the box sequentially, the transparencies will be ready the next time you need them for a similar workshop.

When you turn on the overhead projector, raise the volume of your voice to compensate for the additional noise that comes from the machine fan. In some projectors the fan never turns off, so you may need to use a microphone to compensate.

Turn the projector off when it's not in use. A vacant light space is disconcerting. Similarly, participants will wonder what more you have to say about a transparency if it remains on the screen after you are through speaking about it. By turning the projector off you refocus participant attention from the screen back to you.

Periodically step away from the projector. Once the overhead transparency is projected, move away from the projector. Step toward the participants to regain contact with them.

If you must point to something on the transparency, try to step back to the screen. The participants' eyes will follow you as you indicate the important information. If you stay at the projector, participants will not know whether to look at you or at what you are pointing to. You can also use a pointer on the stage of the overhead projector. If you lay a pen on the overhead transparency to point to the concept, the shadow will project on the screen. Be certain to move away from the projector so that everyone can easily see the screen.

Never walk or stand between the overhead projector and the screen, letting the projected image appear on your body. Not only will the light blind you, but your silhouette will be projected onto the screen. Either walk in front of the overhead projector or turn the projector off when you move to the other side.

Use water-soluble pens during the presentation to check off, circle, or otherwise enclose or underline items you are talking about. The addition of color as well as your action in marking the transparencies will provide variety and focus the participants' attention. Use running water to wash the transparencies off after the presentation. You can also make markings on a clear acetate sheet overlay to save the transparencies from accidental damage.

Reveal items on the transparency as you discuss them. Use a file folder or piece of paper to mask what you have not yet discussed. As you want to disclose additional information, move the paper down on the transparency. Put the paper under the transparency, between it and the glass, so that the paper won't be blown off as you near the bottom.

There is more to using an overhead projector than turning on the machine and projecting a transparency. This section has outlined some general guidelines for producing overhead projections and using them to their fullest potential and greatest advantage in your workshop.

Slides

The photographs that make up a slide presentation can bring teachers right into your classroom to validate what you are sharing. But a slide presentation can also be a signal for some of the participants to take a rest. You'll want to make your slides engage the viewers rather than allow them an excuse to think about something else.

Before you decide whether to include a slide presentation in your workshop, consider the following advantages and disadvantages of the medium.

Advantages
- Slides can easily be seen by large groups.
- Slides can give the participants a clearer understanding of what you are describing because they can show real people in real situations.
- It is fairly easy to make professional-looking slides.
- After the slides are arranged in the projector, showing them is simply a matter of turning the projector on and pressing the advance button.
- It's easy to rearrange slides as the content and participants require.

Disadvantages
- Slides are most effective in a completely darkened room, making eye contact between the facilitator and participants impossible— and participants' reactions difficult to monitor.
- There is usually little interruption and discussion until the slides are finished and the lights are turned on again.
- Slides tend to jam in the projector.
- Remote control mechanisms are not very sturdy or reliable.
- When a bulb burns out in the projector, the machine has to be opened in the middle of a presentation and the bulb removed in order to get a new light source.

Effective Slide Presentations

In order to capitalize on the reasons for including a slide presentation in the workshop, of course, you must make your slides worth viewing.

Here are some specific production and presentation suggestions that will increase the likelihood that your slide presentation will be of interest to the participants:

Plan to make a slide change about once every six to ten seconds. Participants need to view slides long enough to have a chance to see and "read" the photograph, but not so long that the image becomes tiresome. Because the participants cannot easily see you as you speak, you need to count on the slides to maintain interest. Estimate the number of slides you will need by timing your presentation script and multiplying the minutes by five or six.

Use all horizontal or all vertical slides. The projector should be in one position for the entire slide presentation. Combinations of horizontal and vertical slides tend to create viewing problems for participants. Because vertical slides need more room top to bottom, the horizontal slides will be positioned too low on the screen for people in the back to see.

Design your slides so that the participants seated the farthest away will have no difficulty seeing them. To test the readability of the slide for the person in the back of the room, hold the slide at arm's length. If you can read it against a bright background, then it will probably be readable to your audience.

Label or number your slides for easier organization. Put all the slides in the tray and view them prior to the workshop to be certain they are correctly placed in the carousel tray. Then put a number or a dot in the upper right-hand corner of each of the slides before removing them from the tray. This will let you see instantly that (all of the slides) are in the proper position the next time you want to give the presentation.

Use photographs with various points of view. A general guideline is to have three photos of the subject: a long shot to provide a frame of reference, a medium shot to focus on the subject, and a close-up to highlight details that require special attention.

Begin with a title slide to remind participants of the reason for the slide presentation. After you have turned off the lights, you should refocus participants' attention, as their concentration has been interrupted by the sudden darkness. A catchy title slide can quickly remind them why they are watching. Title slides are easily made with computers by printing the text and any graphic onto a piece of acetate in a laser printer.

Think of an uninspiring slide presentation you've watched. List the reasons for your boredom (if you can remember before you fell asleep!). Keep this list handy as you plan your own slide presentation, so that you will not make the same mistakes.

Vary your narration and the slides so that all slides are not showing a single idea. One of the main reasons that a slide presentation can get boring is because the format is always the same—a slide is shown and then described, another slide is shown and described. Consider using several slides to show a single idea and have one slide be an illustration for several follow-up ideas. Variety maintains interest.

Looking Like a Pro with Slides

If you decide that a slide presentation is appropriate for your workshop, you should take certain steps in advance to ensure that your program runs smoothly.

Arrive early and make certain that you know how to switch the projector on and off. If you don't have a remote to control the power, ask one of the teachers in the workshop to turn the projector on and off at your signal.

Locate the light switches and identify which need to be turned off for viewing the slides. If the light switches are far away from where you will be standing (it seems that they always are), then ask someone in the workshop to turn off the lights at your signal.

Be certain that the slide projector has an extra bulb and know where it is. If you are using a type of slide projector you have never used before, practice changing the bulb. You'll want to know the exact procedure should the bulb burn out during the presentation.

Use a carousel slide tray for 80 slides rather than one for 140. Eighty slides are plenty for the participants to view at one time, and the larger-format tray often sticks.

Always put the plastic lock ring on top of the tray after the slides are loaded. The ring will keep the slides in place should the carousel tray accidentally fall.

Know how to remove the tray in case one of the slides jams during the presentation. Use a coin to turn the plastic screw in the center top of a carousel slide projector. This releases the tray so it can be removed. Take the damaged slide out of the projector. Turn the slide tray over and move the metal bottom back to the beginning. Replace the slide tray, advance it to the position where the slide stuck, and continue the presentation.

Use plastic slide mounts to decrease the likelihood of jammed slides. Cardboard slide mounts are cheaper, but they are likelier to jam in the projector.

Set up the projector so that it creates the largest image possible, filling the screen. Be sure all slides are in focus and no one will be sitting in the light path from the projector to the screen.

Place the screen as high as possible. The screen needs to be at least 2 feet above the floor in order to be clearly visible. You may need to put the screen on risers to increase its height.

Project the slides in advance of the presentation to be certain that they are in the tray correctly and are in the right order. An upside-down or backwards slide is unnerving and interrupts the flow of the presentation.

Use black slides for smoother beginnings and endings. When you begin with a black slide, you can turn on the projector and move to the front of the room, if necessary, without having an image on the screen. End with a black slide as well, to avoid shocking the participants with blinding lights. Some recent projector models leave the screen dark when no slide is being projected, thereby eliminating the need for a black slide.

Stand next to the screen while the slides are shown. Position yourself at an angle at the front of the room, mostly facing your audience but slightly toward the screen. This maintains your presence as the facilitator. Use a remote with an extra-long cord if necessary in order to be able to stand near the screen.

Leave a light on if possible. It becomes tedious and difficult for participants to listen to a voice from the dark; a light helps participants maintain contact with you as you are speaking.

Vary the pacing of the slides. Allow ten to twenty seconds per slide, and never project a slide for longer than necessary. If a single concept is going to be discussed for a longer period of time, show two or three slides illustrating the same idea in different ways or from different points of view. Use a series of fast images as a change of pace.

Always carry duplicates of your slides. If a slide is jammed in the projector, you can replace it right away with the duplicate, and it will be ready for the next presentation as well.

Avoid showing slides right after lunch. The combination of a big meal and a dark room is certain to encourage a brief attention span.

Specific suggestions for using slides to increase the enthusiasm for and understanding of the concepts presented in a workshop are described in this section. Used appropriately and imaginatively, slides can bring wonderful photographs of other environments as well as compelling graphics into the workshop setting.

Flip Charts

Flip charts are popular for workshops and small meetings. They consist of a large pad of paper and a stand or easel. Flip charts can be prepared in advance, composed during the workshop to record participants' ideas, or a combination of both.

Advantages
- Flip charts are useful for small group presentations.
- The flip chart paper and stand are both inexpensive.
- Flip charts can be adapted to a variety of situations.
- Flip charts can be made as participants speak, addressing the specific needs of a particular audience.

- Flip charts made during a workshop foster a feeling of collaboration between the facilitator and the participants.
- There is no need for special lighting with flip charts.
- Flip charts are helpful organizers for the workshop because the pages are in sequential order.
- It is easy to save the group work recorded on flip chart pages.

Disadvantages
- Flip charts are difficult to save and reuse; because they are most often meant to be expendable, they are not very durable.
- The person writing on the flip chart needs to have good handwriting.
- The facilitator usually cannot have eye contact with the participants and write at the same time.
- Large groups cannot see flip charts.
- Flip chart tablets are awkward to carry around.
- It takes a particular skill to make the flip charts look neat and organized.
- The flip chart is basically a sequential medium because the pages are turned over as they are used.
- Flip charts require a high input of the facilitator's energy, as they are not usually effective without accompanying narrative.

Producing Effective Flip Charts

Flip charts are best used for the sequential presentation of information to a small group. They are effective when done well but can be confusing and inappropriate in certain situations. What follows are a few guidelines for flip charts:

Make sure the headlines are clear and comprehensive. Headlines should clearly explain the subject of the information on the chart, as shown in Figure 10.2.

Use a variety of styles for your letters. Use ALL CAPS FOR HEADLINES, lowercase for details, *italics for variety,* and <u>underline for emphasis.</u>

Figure 10.2
Headline on flip chart

Highlight key points. Use shadows, boxes, underlines, and stars to focus on words or numbers. Add borders and geometric shapes to add interest. (See Figure 10.3.)

Use bright, bold colors. Pastels should be used only for highlighting. Avoid red except for emphasis, as it is difficult to see from a distance.

Change colors for variety, but use the colors systematically. Choose one color for page headings, one for main points, and another for subpoints.

Distinguish between different types of lists. Use bullets in front of items that are listed in no sequential order, as in Figure 10.4; use numbers to indicate relative importance or order of ideas, as in Figure 10.5.

Include simple cartoons and graphics. Learn to draw basic cartoons that can be done quickly to add to the variety of information on the chart.

Use cutouts as a part of page layout for flip charts. Cut pictures from magazines or shapes from construction paper and paste them to the flip chart pages for variety.

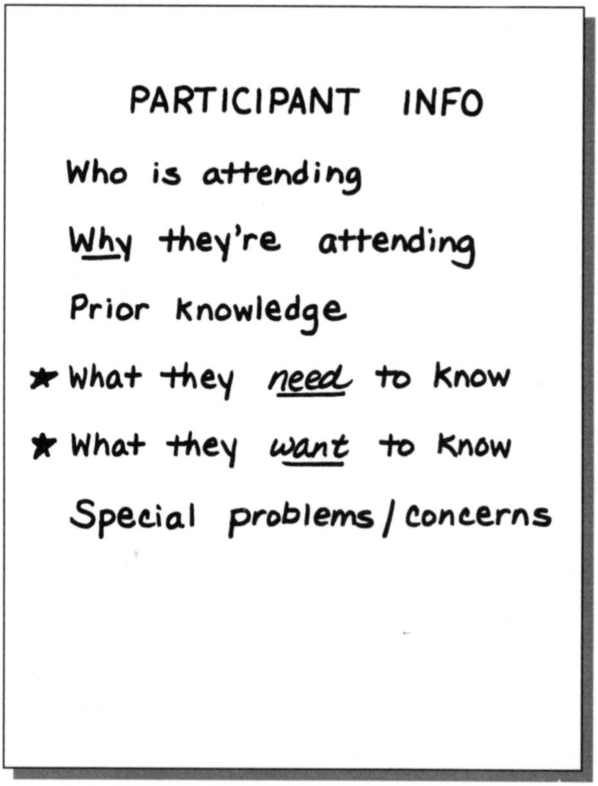

Figure 10.3
Use of stars

After you've determined that the size of your group is appropriate and you know how to produce professional-looking pages, familiarize yourself with the following techniques for using the flip chart.

Rehearse with your charts and know how to use them prior to the workshop. Practice turning the pages smoothly and stepping aside as you speak.

Make sure the easel is securely locked and balanced and that the pad is firmly anchored on the easel. Lean on the easel before using it in the workshop so that you know it will not collapse under the weight of your arm.

Use watercolor markers that do not bleed through to the next page. Write with the broad side of the pen to make letters bold enough for everyone to see.

Write legibly and do not crowd the chart. Letters should be approximately 3 inches high for easier visibility. Claire Raines (1989) has an even more precise formula: letters should be 1 inch high for every 15 feet between the visual and the people sitting in the back of the workshop.

Use symbols and abbreviations in order to write more quickly. When you write quickly you won't have your back to the audience for too long. Be sure to explain the meaning of any unusual symbols and abbreviations.

If you have difficulty writing in a straight, horizontal line, use pads with lines approximately 1 inch apart. It is much easier to read a horizontal line of

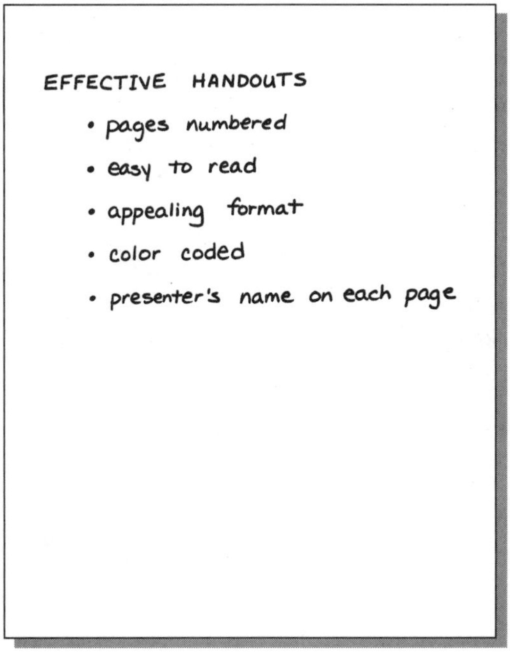

EFFECTIVE HANDOUTS
- pages numbered
- easy to read
- appealing format
- color coded
- presenter's name on each page

TOPIC INFORMATION SEARCH
1. Identify your topic
2. Read about your topic
3. Talk to experts in your topic area
4. Identify personal experiences
5.

Figure 10.4 *Use of bullets*

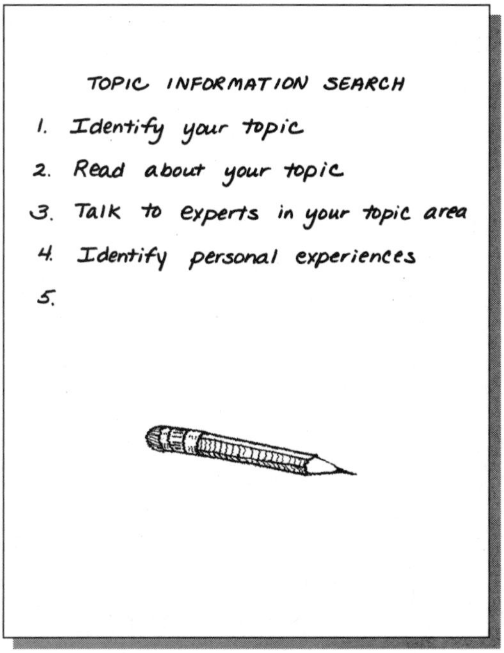

Figure 10.5 *Use of numbers*

words than words that are in a curved line. The lines on the ruled pads are not visible from a distance and will make the flip charts look more professional.

Lightly pencil in advance the information you plan to write on the flip chart during the workshop. The draft helps organize the flip chart yet the light pencil line won't show, so the use of the chart still looks spontaneous. You can also make notes to yourself in pencil at the top corner of the flip chart to help you remember key points you want to make. Previously sketched-in graphics further help every facilitator look like an artist.

Leave the bottom third of the page blank. Everyone, including people sitting in the back, will be able to see all of the information if you write only on the top two-thirds of the page. This also leaves some space if you need to go back and add information to a page later.

Leave a blank page or two between pre-prepared pages. When you have blank pages interspersed with the predrawn pages, you can turn the page without revealing what is coming next. You will also have plenty of space for participants' input; if they have more than one page of ideas to share, you can turn to the next page without coming to your prewritten material.

If there's a page you'll want to use often, make a masking tape tab for the page that precedes it. Flip over the page with the tab on top of it to reveal quickly the page you want.

Prepare some charts in advance, and cover basic ideas with strips of paper that can easily be removed when you are speaking to that point. This masking technique makes it possible to share a flip chart page without giving away all of the important information at once.

Wait at least twenty to thirty seconds after you finish writing before you turn the page. The waiting time gives teachers an opportunity to read, reflect, and take notes.

Stand to the side of the flip chart as you speak to avoid blocking the participants' view. Talk to the participants, not the chart.

Tear off pages by tugging sharply at one corner. Avoid tearing straight down, as this tends to rip the paper.

Flip charts are a well-established visual medium for workshops and presentations. Part of their popularity is due to their relative ease of production and the amount of interaction between the participants and the facilitator that the flip charts encourage. This section covers specific suggestions to increase the likelihood that your flip charts will be an asset to your workshop, both in terms of production techniques and strategies for utilization.

Video

Videotapes and videodiscs are becoming more popular in workshops as the technology becomes more widely available. The number of different videodisc titles is increasing dramatically, and many are appropriate for workshops. Many people have a video recorder at home and are comfortable with its use in workshops.

There are many excellent instructional videotapes and videodiscs that may have a place in your workshop, but consider the advantages and disadvantages of this medium before you decide to include it.

Advantages

- Video is attention-getting and persuasive.
- Video is a quick way to provide a common experience.
- Video shows process and motion.
- Video provides the participants an opportunity to hear important concepts from the experts who developed them.
- Video involves the viewers emotionally and intellectually.
- Participants can view the video many times for review.
- Video can show information from other media, such as films, slides, overhead transparencies, photographs, and graphics.
- Prerecorded videocassettes and videodiscs are easy to use.
- Participants can view the video recordings during breaks as a supplement to or review of key concepts in the workshop.
- Segments of a video can be used to reinforce concepts or demonstrate processes; the entire video does not need to be viewed.
- Information on videodiscs is simple to quickly access with the use of frame search and chapter search.
- Motion image sequences on videodiscs can be slowed down, allowing participants an opportunity to view a particular skill in slow motion for greater comprehension.

Disadvantages

- Because individual images are in view for only a short period of time, they may be hard to recall.
- Video production is difficult and costly.
- Participants will expect a professional video with the same technical quality they see in movies and on television.
- Video is only suitable for a small group unless several monitors or projectors are used.

- Renting the necessary projection equipment for video can be expensive.
- Video is inflexible in that not all of what is on the tape or disc will relate to your workshop, but you will probably have to use the information in the format and at the pace used in the video.
- Video does not readily accommodate responses from participants; they will tend to view the entire program before making comments rather than discuss individual situations.
- Participants may be lulled into viewing passively, in much the same way that people watch television at home.

Looking Like a Pro with Video

Select a video that is compatible with the workshop topic. If the topic of the workshop is related to teaching children, videos selected should feature children. If a video is used on the same topic of the workshop but was designed for a different audience, be sure to consider how its content can be adapted for your particular workshop.

Request a remote for the video equipment. A remote control will allow you to stop and start the recording for discussion without having to bend down in front of the playing equipment. You can often control the brightness, color, and hue of the picture with the remote as well.

Play the video recording just prior to the beginning of the workshop. By starting the video just before the workshop, you will know how to operate the equipment and can be certain that the recording in the machine is the one you intend to use.

Room lights should be left on at approximately half their full power. The room needs to be dark enough for participants to see the picture but light enough for them to take notes. You will also want to be able to see their reactions to the video.

Have the video set for viewing before the workshop participants are in the room. Set the volume and adjust the picture. When it is time to run the video recording, all you should need to do is push the play button.

Use multiple monitors for groups of more than twenty-five people. There should probably be one monitor for every twenty to twenty-five people, placed at appropriate viewing locations.

Prepare the participants for the content of the video. Like your students, participants in your workshop need to have some specific reason for watching a video actively rather than passively. Provide them with a focus for their viewing prior to beginning the video recording.

It is likely that any video you would use in your workshop would be one that was professionally produced. You have probably already used videotapes in your classroom. But there is more to sharing a video than turning on the monitor, if you want to maximize its potential in your workshop.

Think about a lesson that you have used with your students that incorporated a video recording. Think about why you selected the specific video, what you did with the students prior to their viewing the video, and what they did after seeing it. Adapt these same strategies when you use video recordings in your workshop.

Consider providing some of your own narration for the video. Turn off the sound and describe the footage yourself. This is an excellent way to adapt the high-quality visuals for the specific content of your workshop and needs of the participants.

Know when to stop the recording for discussion. Be familiar with the content of the video; preview it before the workshop so that you know the exact content and have identified points at which you want to stop it.

Debrief the participants after viewing the video. Provide an opportunity for participants to discuss various parts of the video, and be ready to replay parts as necessary for the discussion.

Video recordings are rapidly becoming a medium of preference in classrooms and other instructional situations. With proper use, video can be an extremely powerful way to share situations that illustrate your good ideas. The possibilities for use of video in your workshops can only grow as the technology becomes more familiar and the products more sophisticated.

In Conclusion

There are several options for presenting visuals during a workshop. Select the medium that best matches your needs as a facilitator and those of the participants in order to effectively communicate the necessary information.

Resources for the Production of Visuals

OVERHEAD TRANSPARENCIES
Microsoft PowerPoint. Redmond, WA: Microsoft Corporation

Polash, Peter. *Aldus Persuasion*. Seattle, WA: Aldus, 1988

Sparks, Jerry D. *Overhead Projection*. Englewood Cliffs, NJ: Educational Technology Publications, 1981

3M Visual Products. *Create Great Transparencies*. Minneapolis, MN: 3M, 1989

SLIDES

Eastman Kodak Company. *Adventures in Existing Light Photography,* Pamphlet AC-44. Rochester, NY: Eastman Kodak Co.

———. *Beginning Creative Photography for Graphic Communications*. Rochester, NY: Eastman Kodak Co., 1979

———. *The Joy of Photography: A Guide to the Tools and Techniques of Better Photography*. Rochester, NY: Eastman Kodak Co., 1981

———. *Planning and Producing Slide Programs*. Rochester, NY: Eastman Kodak Co., 1977

Green, Lee. *Creative Slide/Tape Programs*. Littleton, CO: Libraries Unlimited, 1986

Podracky, John R. *Creating Slide Presentations: A Basic Guide*. Englewood Cliffs, NJ: Prentice-Hall, 1983

VIDEO

Andersen, Yvonne. *Make Your Own Animated Movies and Videotapes*. Boston: Little, Brown, 1991

Bergman, Robert E. and Moore, Thomas V. *Managing Interactive Video/Multimedia Projects*. Englewood Cliffs, NJ: Educational Technology Productions, 1991

Caiati, Carl. *Video Production—The Professional Way*. Blue Ridge Summit, PA: Tab Books, 1985

Le Baron, John. *Making Television: A Video Production Guide for Teachers*. New York: Teachers College Press, 1981

Millerson, Gerald. *Video Production Handbook*. Boston: Focal Press, 1983

Smith, David L. *Video Communication: Structuring Content for Maximum Program Effectiveness*. Belmont, CA: Wadsworth Publishing, 1990

Works Cited and Suggested Readings

Elliott, Geoff. *Video Production in Education and Training*. Dover, NH: Croom Helm, 1984

Green, Lee. *501 Ways to Use the Overhead Projector.* Illus. by Don
Dengerink. Littleton, CO: Libraries Unlimited, 1982

Heinich, R.; Molenda, M.; and Russell, J. *Instructional Media and the New
Technologies of Instruction.* Chapters 5 and 8. New York: Macmillan, 1993

Jeffries, Janet R.; and Bates, Jefferson. *The Executive's Guide to Meetings,
Conferences and Audiovisual Presentations.* New York: McGraw-Hill, 1986

Kemp, Jerrold E. *Planning and Producing Audio Visual Materials.* 5th ed.
New York: Harper & Row, 1989

Locatis, Craig N.; and Atkinson, Francis D. *Media and Technology for
Education and Training.* Chapters 6, 7, and 9. Columbus, OH: Merrill,
1984

Meilach, Dona Z. "Overhead Transparencies Designed to Communicate."
Arts & Activities (May 1992): 42–43, 50, 52, 56

Pike, Robert W. *Creative Training Techniques Handbook.* Chapter 4.
Minneapolis, MN: Lakewood Books, 1989

Publish It! Easy. Deerfield, IL: Timeworks

Raines, Claire. *Visual Aids in Business.* Section 3. Los Altos, CA: Crisp,
1989

Satterthwaite, Les. *Instructional Media: Materials Production and Utilization.*
2d ed. Dubuque, IA: Kendall/Hunt, 1990

Seaman, Don F.; and Fellenz, Robert A. *Effective Strategies for Teaching
Adults.* Chapter 3, 75–77. Columbus, OH: Merrill, 1989

Simonson, Michael; and Volker, Roger. *Media Planning and Production.*
Chapters 8 and 11. Columbus, OH: Merrill, 1984

Volker, Roger; and Simonson, Michael. *Media for Teachers.* Chapter 4.
Dubuque, IA: Kendall/Hunt, 1989

11

Insurance for Effective Workshops: Seeing to the Last-Minute Details

Think about what you do prior to the first day of school in a new school year or semester. Identify the details you attend to and the final plans you make. Which of these preparations for your classroom would be appropriate to do just before beginning a workshop? You probably indicated that you arrange the classroom, complete displays, and practice what you're going to say. Many of these same last-minute details—and some others unique to the workshop format—will need to be addressed before you begin your workshop.

Attention to last-minute details can give you an edge in making your workshop work for both you and the participants.

Practicing the Workshop

It may be helpful to run through such high-impact parts of your workshop as the opening and closing. Don't overdo the practicing, though. You'll want to remember the sequence of points in your workshop, but you don't want your presentation to sound memorized, which could make it boring. Be familiar with what you want to say yet flexible enough so that you can stray from your plan to take advantage of opportunities (responding to an idea, answering a question, focusing on a particular topic, etc.) that come from the participants.

One effective way to prepare for the workshop is to go through the entire presentation so that you are comfortable with the sequence, including the use of visuals. This run-through can be silent or oral. If you choose to rehearse parts of the workshop aloud, you can follow a number of tactics.

Mirror, Mirror

Standing before the mirror and presenting helps you to see your gestures, giving you the opportunity to identify and adjust your body language. However, don't let this technique trap you into thinking that you're presenting for yourself rather than the participants.

Tape Recorder

Listening to yourself on tape can be an effective way to determine how your voice sounds and to get a sense of your pacing with no visual distractions. Using a tape recorder gives you the chance to practice breath control to vary how your voice sounds. If you are self-conscious about your tape-recorded voice, though, don't try this practice technique. You may overreact to minor problems and lose some of your confidence.

Video Camera

Video recording your presentation gives you an opportunity to view your body language as well as hear your voice. Don't worry if you don't sound like a professional immediately; use this video recording as a tool to help you improve.

If your workshop seems boring when you hear it on tape or watch it on video, it may mean that you need the energy from the audience for motivation. Try audio and video recording in front of an audience for a more accurate experience.

Friendly Critic

Sometimes a close friend or family member can provide some useful insights into your presentation style. Be certain that the critic knows what you are trying to do: critics with a different background from that of your participants may not understand your aims and could give you incorrect or inappropriate feedback. Ask the critic to focus on a particular part of your presentation that you're especially concerned about, such as your use of gestures or your movement around the room.

Checking the Workshop Facility

Practiced workshop facilitators know the value of getting to the workshop early and being fully prepared long before the workshop is ready to begin. In order to be ready for the inevitable and the unexpected, check out the workshop facility early enough so that you have time to make any necessary changes.

Locate thermostat and ventilation controls and learn how to adjust them. Set a comfortable room temperature, considering that the greater the number of people, the more their body heat will affect the temperature.

Familiarize yourself with lighting controls. Know where the banks of lights are located and which switches correspond to specific lights.

Test all video and audio equipment. Be certain that all equipment is in working order and that visuals can be seen from all areas of the room. Have extra light bulbs available for each piece of equipment.

Test the microphone to be certain your voice can be heard in all parts of the room. Know how to adjust the volume. It may be a good idea to request a lavaliere or cordless microphone so that your hands are free and you can move around easily and naturally.

Be certain you have all necessary materials for the overhead projector. Have extra acetate to write on, plenty of water-soluble pens, and appropriate material to clean the projector.

Set up a small clock that is easy to read. It is important that you know the time, but you don't need to draw attention to it. A quick glance at a small clock near where you're standing is much more subtle than turning your wrist to look at your watch.

Hang any posters, charts, or visuals, and be sure they can be seen clearly from any location in the room. Masking tape is usually not strong enough to hold materials on the wall for the entire workshop. If pushpins are not appropriate, use a gummy adhesive.

Set up displays and be certain that they are accessible, with plenty of room for people to browse. A label and brief description always help teachers put the examples into context.

Check the furniture to see that it is adult-sized and appropriate for the activities you have planned for the workshop. Uncomfortable furniture can be very tiring.

Arrange the room and furniture to best suit your workshop. Move furniture so that there is enough space between rows and tables so people can move easily and not interfere with materials. Leave enough space for people to sit while someone else is passing by in front or behind them. If furniture cannot be moved, adapt your workshop to the facilities available.

Clear the aisles so that you can move about as necessary. It is important that you be able to circulate throughout the room. Several aisles may be more appropriate than a single aisle, depending upon the size of the workshop. More aisles also give you the opportunity to have proximity with more participants.

If appropriate, have pleasantly displayed refreshments with such extras as real cream, tablecloths, and herb teas. Teachers need and enjoy a snack during a workshop. In addition to the standard coffee and water, provide some unexpected options—fresh fruit instead of cookies, for example.

Determine whether there are any preset times for breaks, the location of rest rooms, and any other housekeeping details. Participants will need to know this information early in the workshop, so share it at the beginning. You may want to post these details on a flip chart or newsprint.

Provide participants with ready access to water. Water on individual tables is best, but at least have pitchers and glasses in a convenient location.

Setting the Tone of the Workshop

Rather than waiting until the last minute to appear, use the time before the start of the workshop to set the tone and help assure a rewarding time for everyone.

Arrive at the workshop early. If possible, be ready to begin thirty minutes prior to the scheduled workshop start, and use the extra time to interact with participants. At the very least, use the last fifteen minutes prior to the beginning of the workshop to welcome the participants.

Greet and mingle with the participants. This is a good opportunity to learn more about the teachers and let them know some informal information about you. Getting acquainted with participants builds rapport and audience support. It can reduce your stress by allowing you to focus on audience members as individuals. At the same time, it allows the participants to become more comfortable with you.

Watch participants as they enter the room. Notice verbal and nonverbal behavior. Ascertain whether the teachers look interested and eager or bored and resistant. Focus your initial attention on those who look enthusiastic; others will join in as they pick up on the support you already have.

Give workshop materials to the participants as they enter or place packets at their tables in the room. Participants will appreciate being given a chance to preview the materials as they wait for the workshop to start.

Provide name tags or place cards to help everyone identify others by name. Not only is it easier to use names, but doing so fosters an amicable, cooperative environment.

Put a greeting on the overhead projector or on the first page of a flip chart. Let the teachers know you're glad they're attending the workshop. A blank screen or blank piece of paper is not a very welcoming sight. Instead, set up a picture of a person or cartoon character waving hello or project a visual that reflects the content of the workshop (if the workshop is about reading, an appropriate welcome image would be of someone engrossed in a book). Quotes from well-known people are also interesting, but a simple "Good Morning!" or "Welcome" along with the title of the workshop on the flip chart or projected on the screen also makes people comfortable (see Figure 11.1). At other times it may be appropriate to have instructions or specific information on the overhead projector or flip chart.

A popular welcome that I use gives the teachers an opportunity to earn a reward. On one overhead projector is a transparency with the words: "Welcome! There will be lots of opportunities for you to receive books to take back to your classroom during this workshop. The first book goes to the person who can find seven pigs in this illustration. Let me know when you have the solution." The picture that contains the pigs is on another overhead projector.

Figure 11.1
A welcome notice

By giving the participants an optional activity to do just as they enter the workshop, you are letting them know that they will be busy during the session. Those who like something to do right away will be satisfied, and those who like to have a few minutes to settle in can choose to get comfortable instead.

Play music for participants to hear as they enter the room. Music is a subtle way to get the room ready. Some teachers may not consciously notice the music, but it does create a comforting atmosphere. Select music that you like (as you will be hearing it most) and that suggests the tone you want to establish. You may choose music that teachers could play in their classrooms or jazz, classical, or new age selections that will appeal to them as adults. Remember that the teachers in the audience will be of different ages, so try to play something that everyone will like.

Start promptly. Beginning more than five minutes after the announced time is not considerate of those who made an effort to be prompt—and sets the wrong tone for the whole session.

Getting Yourself Set for the Workshop

Even the most experienced workshop facilitator gets nervous just before the workshop begins. This nervousness is a good sign. A little anxiety heightens the facilitator's awareness of what needs to be done in order to make the workshop a success. Experienced facilitators say that when they stop being anxious, they'll stop facilitating workshops.

Dorothy Sarnoff (1981) suggests a facilitator attitude adjustment technique before a presentation. She says to say something to yourself to get ready and build self-confidence:

- "I know what I know" indicates that you've done all you could to prepare for the workshop and you have confidence.
- "I'm glad I'm here" locates you physically in the room and gets you mentally on your own side.
- "I'm glad you're here" helps you remember that the participants are the reason you are presenting the workshop.
- "I care about you" removes your attention from yourself and puts it on the participants. This change in focus can help relieve self-consciousness.

Any sort of positive reinforcement is very helpful just before you enter the workshop facility. My husband always tells me, "Don't forget to smile a lot," and I have found that this simple statement has propelled me through many unexpected situations. Another favorite of mine is "I will still be alive tomorrow no matter what happens today." Identify your own "balance sentences," those statements that you or someone close to you makes that will help relieve some of your preliminary workshop anxiety. Some people find that carrying an inspirational motto or reading with them activates their courage and motivation.

Remember that people who have decided to take part in the workshop want you to succeed, and most will do what they can to make that success possible. After all, they wouldn't purposely attend something with the idea that it would fail. So . . .

- Put one foot in front of the other.
- Imagine a relaxing, happy place.
- Feel a strong hand on your shoulder.
- Imagine yourself poised and in control.
- Say to yourself, "I'm terrific at this."
- Greet them with a smile.

In Conclusion

After you have fully planned and prepared your workshop, concentrate on the details: practicing the presentation, preparing the workshop facility, and setting the workshop tone. Each of these areas of concern, as well as last-minute details to get *yourself* ready, can be key factors in the success of your workshop.

Works Cited and Suggested Readings

Pike, Robert W. *Creative Training Techniques Handbook.* Minneapolis, MN: Lakewood Books, 1989

Sarnoff, Dorothy. *Make the Most of Your Best.* New York: Doubleday, 1981

Smith, Terry C. *Making Successful Presentations: A Self-Teaching Guide.* 2d ed. Chapters 7 and 8. New York: John Wiley & Sons, 1991

G O

Education is above all the giving
of examples through actions.
—Paulo Freire

You've planned the workshop, and the teachers have arrived. In this section, you'll find some guidelines to help you as the workshop is in progress and some helpful hints regarding evaluation of the session.

★ ★ ★ ★

12

Communicating with the Workshop Participants

How you communicate with your participants can make the difference between appearing committed to and enthusiastic about the workshop and its topic or seeming simply to go through the motions. Both verbal and nonverbal communication have a significant impact on the total workshop experience.

Verbal Communication

The workshop facilitator's voice affects how the participants will relate to the facilitator and perceive what is said. You must sound genuine and talk to, not at, the teachers attending the workshop.

Pay attention to the sound of your voice. Vary the volume, pitch, and tone to emphasize critical points in the workshop. Note whether your voice goes up at appropriate times. Be sure that everyone can hear and that your voice doesn't fade; if you need a microphone, use it. Plan to ask someone in the back of the room to give you a subtle signal if your voice fades and you can no longer be heard. At times during the workshop you'll want to speak loudly; at other times you can almost whisper to draw the participants into what you are saying. Learn to use the sound of your voice to maximize the impact of what you're saying.

Determine your natural pace of speaking. You'll want to be fast enough to sound enthusiastic and

Listen to well-known speakers on prerecorded tapes. Listen for inflection, rate, enunciation, volume, and so on. Note what enhances their presentation. Then make a tape recording of your voice by turning on the tape recorder as you are presenting a lesson to your students. Compare your presentation to that of the professionals (don't be too hard on yourself). What can you do to improve the effectiveness of your voice?

slow enough to be understood. A fast speaker conveys enthusiasm but can be tiring to listen to for long periods of time. Share key words and concepts slowly and describe less important materials more rapidly.

Learn to pause after saying things you want the participants to weigh carefully. A pause gives the teachers time to understand and think about what has been said. Don't be anxious about periods of silence during the workshop; they are often a signal that participants are thinking about concepts or ideas presented.

Use language that is appropriate for the participants. Although the use of jargon and current expressions may seem timely, don't let the language get in the way of the communication. Be certain that you know the correct pronunciation of technical or difficult words, and define terminology that may be new to some participants.

The sound of your voice greatly influences the way you communicate with participants in the workshop. Be sure that your volume, pacing, and tone are giving the same message as the words you are saying.

Nonverbal Communication

It's been said that *how* you say something is as important as *what* you say. Nonverbal cues tell the participants a lot about what you're saying, so be certain that your nonverbal language doesn't negate your verbal communication. Controlling your nonverbal signals isn't always easy, but you can learn to accentuate their positive aspects.

Maintain eye contact to establish communication channels and build rapport with the participants. One experienced workshop facilitator says that one of the best compliments she received was from a woman who began a letter with, "You probably remember me. I sat in the sixth row. I had on a blue dress and was in the third seat from the aisle." Of course there was no way the facilitator could remember that woman out of a group of over 1,500 teachers, but she was flattered that the teacher thought she did. Eye contact established the connection between the two, and it made a definite impression on the participant.

Don't just look at the teachers; see them. Seek out someone in each section of the room (preferably someone who seems to be enjoying the workshop), and focus long enough to draw that teacher in, but not so long as to make him feel uncomfortable.

Be aware of your body language. Gestures and animation are personal. If you know your subject and believe in what you are saying, your gestures will be natural. Look in the mirror to determine which of your gestures invite positive responses and which gestures you want to avoid because of the possible negative impression they could convey. Because I tend to wave my hands around a lot when I speak, I always try to wear something with pockets. While I don't want to keep my hands in my pockets all of the time, they are available when I need to control myself.

Move throughout the workshop setting. The participants sitting in the back of the room want to know that you're aware of their presence. Move through the room while you're talking, and when the participants are working. When you stand closer to people, they have a greater investment in the workshop.

Avoid separating yourself from the participants by using a desk, lectern, or a podium. If you need to have notes, place them on a table and pick them up to refer to them when participants are engaged in other activities.

Communication is an interactive process. Pay attention to the participants attending the workshop, just as they pay attention to you. Look for their reactions to what you are saying to help you gauge their understanding and feeling toward the workshop. Use the participants' nonverbal communication as they use yours—as a way to understand the underlying message.

Humor

Humor can maintain participants' interest; laughter can make everyone comfortable and encourages camaraderie. Not every workshop facilitator is good at (or should even try) telling canned jokes, but a sincere, natural humor is wonderful for warming up a workshop.

Humor from your own experience is genuine, effective, and always at hand. It makes you look human and brings the group together as the participants identify with the trials and triumphs. An added bonus is that the teachers won't have heard the anecdote if it's based upon your personal experience.

Laugh lines—every teacher has them. Think of a funny event that occurred in your classroom. Write it down. A laughter log of those situations that all of us have experienced or dread experiencing—the kind that all of us can understand—will become a treasure trove of anecdotes to tell in your workshop.

Use only humor that emphasizes your point. Making people laugh for no good reason can become tedious. Let topic-related cartoons, stories, anecdotes, and puns reinforce points throughout your presentation. (Although the bibliography at the end of this book is primarily geared to children, the books in this list are great sources for humorous stories and poems that you could add to your repertoire for adult workshops.)

Take advantage of spontaneous opportunities to laugh during the workshop. During a recent children's literature workshop, teachers were evaluating children's books. One teacher was especially engrossed in a book during an independent reading time. Someone else was looking for a particular book by Maryann Kovalski. It was nowhere to be found, so I asked aloud, "Who has *Pizza for Breakfast?*" The teacher who was immersed in the book proclaimed loudly, "I do. This morning I had pepperoni and sausage." Naturally, everyone began laughing, and this teacher who had been a little bit on the perimeter of the class turned slightly red, began laughing uncontrollably, and became an integral part of the group.

Avoid humor that might offend or alienate participants. It's okay to poke fun at yourself, but never joke at the expense of any of the participants. And of course never tell an inappropriate joke or one that may be construed as such. Because your participants are adults does not mean that anything you say will be acceptable or accepted.

Use the kind of humor that comes most naturally to you, and use it appropriately throughout the workshop. Workshop facilitators able to use humor effectively are those who do so naturally. Learn to laugh at yourself; it makes you look human and puts the participants at ease. Further, it shows that you are comfortable with the group and self-confident about what you do. Some of the humor comes with experience and confidence, but watch carefully for those spontaneous moments when everyone can have a good laugh. Unless you tell jokes very well, leave the canned jokes to the professional comedians and share your personal humor instead.

Question-and-Answer Techniques

Questions are integral to effective workshops; they are an important way for participants to glean and clarify the information they want. Some facilitators even mistakenly look to participant questions as a gauge for their enthusiasm; if there are no questions, these facilitators assume there is little interest. This is not necessarily true, but you *should* do what you can to elicit questions.

Individual Questions

Certain actions encourage individual participants to ask questions:

Step toward the participants, raise your hand, and then ask for questions. By moving into the group, you are becoming more accessible. By raising your hand, you are using the visual signal for questions, and the teachers will follow your lead and raise their hands with their questions.

Assume that there are questions. Do not rush the questions. In all likelihood, not everything you described or the teachers did was perfectly clear to everyone. Allow thinking time before assuming that there are no questions.

If there are no questions immediately, ask the first question yourself. Think of a question teachers usually ask in a similar workshop, ask it of yourself, and then answer it. This shows that you are serious about answering questions and gives the teachers a model for asking their own questions. Begin by saying something like, "Teachers usually ask how they can find time in their already overcrowded curriculum to include what I am sharing today." Answer that question, then let the teachers follow your example.

Wait until the questioner has finished with the entire question before you begin your answer. Although you think you have heard the question before, it may have a different context, and you owe the participant the respect of listening to the whole question. You also want to give yourself plenty of time to think through an appropriate response.

Repeat and rephrase the question. A restatement makes certain that all of the participants hear the question and verifies your understanding of it.

Listen for the intent as well as the content of the question. Try to determine what the teacher is really asking. Watch as the question is asked; there may be some strong nonverbal clues as to the intensity of the question, the feelings behind it, or any hidden agendas.

Answer the question completely and accurately, without going off on a tangent. Give the question the attention it deserves, but don't use it to go off in your own direction. If you do stray from the topic, participants will forget what the question was and will wait for you to get back to the workshop topic rather than listen to what you have to say.

Determine how much of an answer the questioner wants. Answer the question thoroughly, but try not to give more information than is really requested or desired. Your answer is complete when the person who asked the question seems satisfied.

If you don't know the answer to the question, admit it and suggest some places where the participant might find the answer. It isn't likely that you will know all of the answers, so don't pretend that you do. Participants will appreciate your honesty and respect you for it. If you can follow through with your promise, you may tell participants that you will research the answer and get back to them.

Involve all of the participants in the answer to the question. Look at the questioner while you respond, but don't neglect everyone else. Look at participants in several parts of the room to engage them in the response as well.

Read the audience to determine when the number of questions needs to be limited. You don't want to lose the majority of the teachers' attention by focusing on questions from a few. Always remind participants that you are available during breaks to answer any additional questions they might have.

Determine the best time for you to answer questions. Some workshop facilitators are more comfortable having a particular time devoted to questions rather than taking them intermittently throughout the day. Others like to have teachers ask the questions when they are timely, which assures that the response will relate to the current topic of the workshop. Listening to answers to questions doesn't require the same amount of concentration from the participants as the regular workshop activities, so consider a brief question-and-answer session as a transition into the workshop after a break. The important thing is to let participants know that their questions are important and will be considered and answered.

Share individual questions with the entire group. If during the break someone asks a question that you think might be of interest to many of the teachers attending the workshop, write the question down and share it along with the answer after everyone has returned from the break.

If there are no questions, move on. If no one asks you a question, you could assume that you have done such an excellent job that all questions have been answered. It may be, though, that participants are too tired, bored, or even overwhelmed to ask a question. Evaluate what you've been doing to determine what needs to be changed to encourage more questions in the future.

Handling the Tough Questions

Every once in a while someone asks a question that isn't easy to answer. The best strategy for handling these difficult questions is to be prepared for them.

Think about reasons the participant may have asked the particular question. If you sense that the questioner is challenging or testing you, suggest that you talk during the break or after the workshop. Seek that person out to discuss the question at the later time.

Pause before responding to allow yourself time to think about the many possible answers to the question. This pause can move you away from a defensive position as you think of examples and stories that you can use to substantiate your answer.

Before you speak, mentally prepare your key points. Think about the impact your response may have on the questioner, on the other teachers, and on the momentum of the workshop.

Check back with the questioner to ensure you answered the question asked.
If the questioner feels put off or thinks you skirted the issue, suggest you talk
further at the break.

Save the questioner's face. Always treat the questioner with respect even if
that respect is not reciprocated. Be careful not to suggest that the question is
ridiculous or that the person hadn't listened when the answer to the question
was shared earlier.

Questions can be the hallmark of interest in a workshop. Use the questions
to review, to introduce new information, and to increase momentum. Questions
are a unique opportunity for workshop participants and facilitator to engage in
a dialog about a subject of interest to everyone.

Transitions

When it is time to move from one topic or activity to another, transitions help
participants maintain and understand the focus of the workshop. Because participants don't have a page in a book to refer back to, facilitators need to provide reference points that connect one idea, strategy, or piece of information to
another. Smooth transitions help teachers make links between what has been
said and done and what is yet to come.

Where Does It All Fit?

Frequently tell participants where the topic fits into the total workshop plan.
Remind them how their activity connects with the topic. Describe, too, how the
workshop topic or activity fits with their classroom activities.

Teasers

Provide teasers letting participants know what is coming later. Comments such
as "I'm going to share one of my favorite activities after the break" will tell
participants why it is important for them to come back to the workshop.

Questions and Answers

Allow participants a few minutes to collect their thoughts and think of questions about the workshop before moving into a new learning cycle. Limit this
time period, and let participants know of the limit before it begins. They can
share the questions in small groups, or you may want to ask for questions from
the total group.

Learning Logs

At various times throughout the workshop, give participants an opportunity to write down what they've learned and questions they still have. This personal reflection gives them time to think about the concepts in the workshop. Writing in their learning logs also helps teachers organize and put their thoughts into writing before sharing them orally with others. In longer workshops, participants can be given time to share their learning log insights with other teachers in the workshop. (See a sample learning log in the Appendix.)

It Has Possibilities, But . . .

Encourage participants to look at all aspects of an idea shared. In their learning logs, they can evaluate an idea, strategy, or piece of information presented— what was positive about the idea, what was negative, and what was intriguing.

Physical Movement

Sometimes the transition that is needed is a stretch break. Participants can be asked to stand up in response to a question or according to the type of response they have written. For example, you might say, "Stand up if you have learned something in this workshop that you can use with your students" or "Stand up if this workshop has validated something you've already done with your students."

Change of Media

Using a different type of media signals a transition to a different part of the workshop. If you have been using overhead transparencies, for example, switch to the flip chart or share student work.

Interesting Puzzles and Games

A variety of puzzles and brief games that are related to the topic can be inserted into the workshop at appropriate times. These provide a switch that allows those who are interested in the puzzle to think about its solution. It also gives some additional processing time to teachers who want to think about ideas and strategies presented.

Review

A brief review identifying the points covered can lead into a new topic. Sometimes the participants can list what has occurred; at other times the facilitator can provide the recap.

Music

Music can signal a change in activity, stimulate group work, or bring the group back after a break. Include various types of music throughout the workshop to appeal to all of your participants. Popular songs tend to liven things up, classical music may establish calm, and new age arrangements can inspire creativity. Choose the type of music that leads into the mood of the new activity or topic.

Transitions are important when the topic or focus of the workshop changes. They help teachers make adjustments between what has been shared and experienced and what is yet to come. Smooth transitions make clear the connections between what has been said and done and the next topic or activity.

Dealing with Difficult People

The easiest workshops to facilitate are those in which all of the participants are happy to be there, eager to learn, and leave feeling satisfied. The reality, however, is that sometimes workshops are not necessarily what we hope they will be. Although the best insurance for a successful workshop is careful and thorough planning, sometimes the best-laid plans go astray.

Unresponsive Groups

SOMETHING ELSE IS ON THEIR MINDS

Most facilitators have had a workshop that just didn't seem to click. The workshop was well planned and prepared, but even the guaranteed ideas, stories, and activities didn't get the expected reaction. When there is no response to what usually works, some outside stimulus is probably tapping the participants' energy; try to find out what. Don't ask the entire group (some may not notice there's a problem), but check with individual teachers to determine if you should know about a particular situation.

I was once facilitating a workshop of teachers and getting absolutely no response. I knew that it was a workshop the teachers were required to attend. However, I also knew that it had been arranged and planned by a group of teachers. In fact, I was asked to do the workshop because some teachers had seen me facilitate another workshop. I was doing everything I knew to generate enthusiasm, but nothing was happening.

During the first break, I asked the person responsible for arranging the workshop what I was doing wrong. She told me the teachers were preparing to go on strike in a couple of days, the culmination of long and bitter negotiations. My first reaction was, "What am I doing here?" Of course the teachers weren't responding: they had more important things on their minds. After the break, I addressed the issue, told them of my personal experiences during a strike, and then encouraged all of us to make the best of the situation. First of all, we couldn't go anywhere. Second, even if the strike did occur, it wasn't going to last forever, and the workshop was full of easy-to-implement strategies that required little planning. While on strike, they would have little time (or desire) for planning, so these ideas were especially relevant for them at this time. The workshop turned around, and they were with me.

Brrrrrrrr

At some time you may have a group of teachers who are just not interacting. Icebreakers (like those found in Chapter 8) are meant for them. They may need really active warm-ups, and more of them than usual. Because a group isn't outgoing doesn't necessarily mean the participants aren't enjoying and learning from the workshop, but it is much easier for the facilitator if the people in the workshop interact with one another.

Prove It to Me

If you sense that the teachers are hostile as they come to the session, talk to individuals to try to discover what's wrong. If the teachers turn hostile during the workshop, it may be because of frustration or confusion. Seek out the reason for the hostility and address it.

zzzzzzzz

If the group is falling asleep, it probably means that you have been doing too much of the talking. Get the teachers actively doing something. Drowsiness is especially prevalent after lunch, so get them moving.

???????

You may have some teachers who, for some reason, just don't seem to understand what you're saying. Try restating the instructions, giving more examples. If they still don't understand, it may be that they are suffering from task avoidance; they're afraid they won't be able to do the task acceptably, the trust level is low (they'll be embarrassed or harassed), or they just don't feel prepared. Refer back to the original aims of the workshop to determine if they are still appropriate, and find out what is really the matter.

Let's Have a Great Time

The teachers might be having a great time, but you're not certain that the workshop is headed where it should be. Try some nonthreatening approaches (reiterating the schedule, for example) to try to get them to return to the task at hand, or lighten up and present your ideas with a little more fun in mind.

MEMBERS ONLY

Cliquish groups are most prevalent in workshops where the teachers know one another and work together. Determine if the cliques are a detriment to the workshop—it may be that the teachers are together because they work best together. If the cliques detract from your purpose, then increase the number of activities in which participants need to work in various groups.

As frustrating as some of these groups can be, the facilitator usually can work with the situation and make the workshop a success. If you have some strategies at the ready, you can usually get at least some of the members of nonresponsive groups to become actively involved.

Disruptive Participants

More difficult than having groups who don't respond is having participants who are dissatisfied with the workshop for any number of reasons and who let their dissatisfaction be known. These people are participating but not in the positive manner that you would hope. Although you may want to ask them to leave, that's not always possible. The most effective way to deal with this problem is to avoid it by offering a well-planned and effectively conducted workshop. However, it is a good idea to have some strategies ready in case there is some negative participation in your workshop.

CHALLENGERS

Some people may challenge what you say with remarks like, "Don't you think that . . . " or "What about a situation when . . . ." These participants may be processing the information and have legitimate questions about the workshop content. Be careful not to become defensive. Rather than responding yourself, turn the question back to the challenger or ask others in the group to respond. If the challenge involves a comparison with a situation or information that is unfamiliar to you, admit it, and ask others for their input. Always offer to talk with the person during the break.

TALKING SUBGROUPS

Sometimes there are groups of teachers who see the workshop as an opportunity to visit with their friends and to catch up on the latest news. Indeed one reason for workshops is to provide opportunities for participants to visit with one another. However, during the workshop is not an appropriate time for people to chat about unrelated issues. To stem the tide of disruptive conversation,

- walk toward the talkers as you speak
- establish eye contact with the conversationalists
- ask the talkers directly if they have any questions
- ask the talkers if they have something they would like to share with the group
- talk with the people during the break

If there is a lot of chatting, stop and give participants an opportunity to talk about an issue. It may be that you did not anticipate a reaction to a particular section of the workshop, and you need to read the audience and deal with what they need at that particular moment.

The One Who Always Has Something to Say

Every once in awhile you'll have someone in your workshop who has something to say about almost everything. Although you want to encourage participation, there is a point beyond which enough is enough. There are some strategies you can use to let these people know that they've said enough:

- Change your position, moving away from the speaker, and returning to the position you had when you began speaking.
- Ask the rest of the participants what they think.
- Refer to the workshop schedule or aims.
- Summarize their comments and continue the workshop.
- Avoid eye contact.
- Give a gentle reminder about the topic.
- Suggest that you will be able to talk during the break or after the workshop.

Perhaps the most helpful thing to remember when facilitating workshops is your training as a classroom teacher. Recall how you respond to your students in the classroom, and use a suitable version of that response with the workshop participants. Your experience gives you the confidence it takes to confront the situation and resolve whatever problem is causing it.

In Conclusion

Communication with participants is a key to a successful workshop. You are sharing information with them and should communicate to find out their responses and needs as related to the workshop content. This two-way communication is both nonverbal and verbal. Additionally, providing appropriate transitions and encouraging questions from participants can help to engage the teachers actively. Strategies for dealing with so-called problem participants are also necessary to make the workshop a meaningful and enjoyable experience for everyone.

Works Cited and Suggested Readings

Davis, Larry Nolan. *Planning, Conducting, and Evaluating Workshops.* Austin, TX: Learning Concepts, 1974

Elgin, S. H. *Staying Well with the Gentle Art of Verbal Self-Defense.* Englewood Cliffs, NJ: Prentice-Hall, 1990

Feigelson, Sheila B. "Boring Meetings? Put Humor to Work!" *Journal of Staff Development,* 8 (Fall 1987): 63–66

Garmston, Robert. "Notes on the Persuasive Art of Presenting: Responding to Questions." *Developer* (March 1991)

Hamlin, Sonya. *How to Talk So People Listen.* Chapters 2, 3, and 8. New York: Harper & Row, 1988

Hanks, Kurt; and Pulsipher, Gerreld. *Getting Your Message Across.* Los Altos, CA: Crisp, 1991

Kohl, Herbert. *A Book of Puzzlements.* New York: Schocken, 1981

Mandel, Steve. *Effective Presentation Skills.* Sections 6 and 7. Los Altos, CA: Crisp, 1987

Pike, Robert W. *Creative Training Techniques Handbook.* Minneapolis, MN: Lakewood Books, 1989

Smith, Terry C. *Making Successful Presentations: A Self-Teaching Guide.* 2d ed. Chapter 10. New York: John Wiley & Sons, 1991

Warnock, Peter. "Humor as a Didactic Tool in Adult Education." *Lifelong Learning,* 12 (August 1989): 22–24

13

Evaluation

Evaluation is essential and valuable for workshop development and improvement. When the evaluation is completed to gather information, to focus on goals, or to identify learning opportunities, it is a useful tool that can help make your next workshop even better. Because many of our experiences with evaluation have been value judgments—students are evaluated with grades; teachers are evaluated to determine whether they should retain their positions—workshop evaluations may, understandably, seem threatening to some facilitators.

Of course everyone wants to be liked and respected. Most workshop facilitators tend to take personally a less than enthusiastic response to a workshop. One of the most common mistakes that facilitators make is to focus all their attention on participants who are critical, overlooking the teachers who are enthusiastic about the workshop. For some reason, negative evaluations are given more credibility than the many positive evaluations about the workshop. Nobody can please all of the people, all of the time, but constructive evaluations can be a tool workshop facilitators can use to get closer to that goal.

Effective Evaluation Strategies

Helpful evaluations are those that provide specific information that can be applied in subsequent workshop planning and development. You can use certain techniques to elicit this sort of constructive criticism.

Ask for what you want to know. If you really only want people to tell you what a great job you did, then do not ask them how the workshop can be improved. Be certain you identify criteria and statements for your evaluation that reflect the specific information you want. As you develop a way for participants to evaluate the effectiveness of the program, consider what you want them to tell you about:

facilities
appropriateness of the content

facilitator's knowledge of the subject
facilitator's interest in participants
handouts
visuals
length of time spent on specific topics
what made the workshop effective
what they would like to change

Be as specific as possible in the evaluations. Asking participants how well they liked the workshop or if they learned anything as a result of attending the workshop may not give you practical feedback. More useful information is gleaned from more specific questions:

- Was there enough variety in the workshop activities? Explain.
- What information or idea will you think about most?
- What was the most useful part of this workshop? Why?
- What was the least useful part of this workshop? Why?
- What made it easy for you to be here today?
- What made it difficult for you to be here today?
- What are some ideas and insights that you have now that you did not have when the workshop began?
- What appreciations/resentments/regrets (choose one) would you like to express before you leave?
- What final statements would you like to make to the workshop facilitator or to other participants?
- Write three to five adjectives that describe your experience in this workshop.
- What was the biggest surprise for you during this workshop?

Notice trends rather than concentrating on specific comments in the evaluations. It is perfectly conceivable that someone could be having a bad day for reasons beyond your control, and no matter what you did, the workshop would not be satisfactory. If only one or two people have a particular comment, do not modify your workshop because of it. However, if the same or similar comments appear on several evaluations, this may be an indication of a trend that calls for a change.

Now that you have identified the questions you want to ask, you'll need to decide when to ask them. A formal evaluation is usually completed at the close of a workshop, but there are plenty of opportunities for evaluation throughout the session. Each type of evaluation, whether concluding or ongoing, has its strengths and benefits and can be extremely helpful to you as you plan any

As you're planning how to evaluate your own workshop, think about what you, as a participant, would like to have told the facilitator of the last workshop you attended. Write these comments and then develop the questions that your comments could answer. Use these questions as a guide for the evaluation form for your workshop; ask the kinds of questions that let the participants give the facilitator some appropriate feedback.

subsequent workshops on similar or different topics.

Concluding Workshop Evaluations

The traditional method of workshop evaluation is for the participants to complete a standard form just prior to the conclusion of the workshop. The facilitator then reads these forms for an indication of the effectiveness of the workshop. Although these forms can provide valuable information for workshop development, they have several limitations.

Opinions and feelings, participants' reactions to the workshop, are often subjective, yet they may become the primary source for a concluding workshop evaluation. A numerical representation of the worth of a workshop can be value-laden and difficult to interpret—some people never give the highest rating while others think almost anything is great. People may even misread the directions and rate the workshop low numerically, when they actually intended to give it the highest rating. Without an agreed-upon rationale that sets a reason for selecting a specific number, the numerical rating is not of much help in suggesting workshop improvement.

Written comments make an evaluation more useful. But because there is little or no opportunity for the facilitator to speak with the evaluator about a specific criticism, many remarks can be misinterpreted. People may also avoid writing them altogether for fear of lack of anonymity.

Nevertheless, as numerical forms can be completed quickly, the return rate is high, and they do provide an overview of the participants' reactions to the workshop. Examples of end-of-workshop evaluation forms appear in the Appendix of this book.

Perhaps the most significant flaw of evaluations completed at the end of the workshop is that there is no opportunity to use the comments of those attending the workshop to better meet their needs: evaluations can be used to improve the next workshop but have no impact on the workshop being evaluated. There is a reason, then, to get participant feedback while the workshop is in progress.

There are some techniques to evaluate the workshop while it is in progress that can lead to improvement during the specific workshop as well as program development for subsequent workshops. Some in-process workshop evaluation techniques can be awkward and interrupt the flow of the workshop; those listed below are less intrusive.

Present planned outcomes and activities at the start of the workshop and give the participants an opportunity to provide input as to content. Using the introduction as a time to share the workshop content provides a forum for a discussion of workshop expectations. Throughout the workshop, refer back to this list to assess how well expectations are being met.

Listen to the participants' comments to one another before and throughout the workshop to glean valuable insights. Teacher participants may say things to one another that they wouldn't say to the workshop facilitator. Be aware of remarks teachers make as they work and during breaks. These informal observations provide some of the best information for program development. Try not to be a snoop, but do listen closely to what the participants are saying.

Watch the participants' actions, behaviors, and body language, looking for enthusiastic interaction and nodding heads to suggest how well the workshop is meeting their needs. Some teachers may involuntarily give you definite signals about their reaction to a statement, an activity, or an idea; their nonverbal language and interaction with one another is a telling gauge.

Pay attention to the amount of participation in the workshop activities and the number of people who are eager to share with others. If participation is waning, take this as a sign that the teachers are either getting tired or the activity is not as motivating as some of the others had been. Be sensitive to the interest level, and change strategies as necessary.

At the beginning of the session, distribute a simple evaluation form for participants to complete and turn in during a break or at lunch. This form can provide feedback about what is working and what could be improved. Review with the participants the key components on which the workshop will be evaluated. Their responsibility is to let you know when the workshop falls below excellence, so that you can make appropriate adjustments. The use of a standardized form increases the likelihood that participants will respond to the same criteria and decreases the chance that the workshop facilitator will misinterpret any signals.

You might also try a midpoint evaluation form that includes the following questions:

- Is the workshop what you expected it would be? If not, indicate how it differs from your expectations?
- Is the workshop facilitator attending to the workshop goals as you understand them? If not, indicate what is not being addressed?
- What are the strengths of the workshop?
- What are the weaknesses of the workshop?

It is necessary to be ready and able to incorporate into the workshop the suggestions you receive in an ongoing evaluation; asking for suggestions and then not using them will discourage participants from providing any additional feedback. Not all ideas, though, need to be implemented; be careful not to let a vocal minority dominate the general opinion. Because in-process evaluations are interactive, you need to share the results and your reactions as well.

Participants' Self-Evaluations

In addition to evaluating the workshop content and the workshop facilitator, participants can evaluate their own learning during the workshop. When they record specifically what they learned, they have a better sense of how valuable the workshop really was for them. This participant evaluation also gives you, the facilitator, an opportunity to determine what the participants perceive they have learned and compare that to your own goals for the workshop.

Personal Reflections

Encourage participants to write comments in their learning logs or notes about the workshop under the following headings:

New ideas I learned at the workshop
Questions raised as a result of my attendance at this workshop
What I'm going to do as a result of having taken this workshop
Feelings I had during the workshop

These notes will help the teachers remember details of the workshop content and increase the likelihood that they will implement some of what they learned.

Sentence Completions

In order to get teachers to reflect on the ideas presented in the workshop and to evaluate their overall experience, ask them to complete the following sentence stems:

In this workshop I learned that . . .
My thinking was reinforced about . . .
I was surprised that . . .
The best part of the workshop was . . .

3-2-1
Participants will also focus on specific applications of their workshop experience by taking a cue from this countdown:

3 important things I've learned

2 ideas or insights I will share with colleagues

1 action I will take immediately

Contributions and Benefits
Participants can also draw up side-by-side lists of what they contributed to the workshop and what they gained from their participation. This reinforces the notion that workshops are a collaboration between the facilitator and all participants, as everyone has expertise to share.

Facilitator's Evaluation

One other important evaluation is your personal assessment of the workshop. Although it is certainly important to receive input from the participants, you should evaluate yourself: identify what you felt good about regarding the workshop and what you would like to improve.

Stars and Questionables
Do a personal debriefing immediately after the workshop, when you best remember what worked really well and what you want to change. Make a quick list of "stars" (*) and "questionables" (?) using the form shown in the Appendix. Complete this form before reading the participants' workshop evaluations, so as not to be unduly influenced by their opinions. Your rationale for liking or not liking a particular workshop activity may be different from the participants', and you don't want to discount your own needs as a facilitator. Complete the form for each workshop, and keep them long enough to determine whether the specific insights reflect a trend or are just the results of bad or good days.

Three Questions

Another technique for self-evaluation is to ask yourself three questions after the workshop is complete.

1. What did I do today that *worked?* (Note that this isn't necessarily the same as what you liked.)
2. What did I do today that didn't work?
3. What should I change?

Your answers to these questions can provide the focus you need to improve your workshop.

Acrostic Analysis

Robert Pike (1989) suggests that an acrostic grid can be appropriate for workshop review. Adapt his technique to have participants evaluate their own learning or summarize the content of the workshop.

Choose a phrase that represents the content of the workshop. Identify topics, one beginning with each letter in the phrase. Figure 13.1 is a sample grid developed to review the content of a workshop about facilitating. Participants rate their knowledge about the identified facilitator skills. They can circle the areas in which they know most and identify those as strengths; similarly, those areas in which they know the least are their areas of greatest need.

You can also use this acrostic to evaluate your own skills as a workshop facilitator. Rate yourself by marking an X under the number that reflects your assessment of your skills for each facilitator trait. Circle the three areas in which you rated yourself highest and record them under greatest strengths; likewise, circle the three characteristics that have the lowest numbers, and list those under greatest needs.

Adapt this model by using your own acrostic and filling in the important characteristics, requirements, or examples of the particular topic. During a workshop, you can provide the acrostic, and participants can fill in the characteristics. Consider using this as an assessment of what participants know and need to know about a subject as well. Without the rating scale, the acrostic serves as an excellent review of workshop content.

In Conclusion

Few people question the importance of workshop evaluation for program development. The discussion in this chapter is primarily concerned with the

Acrostic Analysis

	Low						High
Skills in communication	1	2	3	4	5	6	7
Hears the participants	1	2	3	4	5	6	7
Adaptable	1	2	3	4	5	6	7
Ready (prepared)	1	2	3	4	5	6	7
Innovative	1	2	3	4	5	6	7
Natural	1	2	3	4	5	6	7
Genuine	1	2	3	4	5	6	7
You'll learn a lot	1	2	3	4	5	6	7
Organized	1	2	3	4	5	6	7
Unique	1	2	3	4	5	6	7
Responsive	1	2	3	4	5	6	7
Giving (of ideas, of self)	1	2	3	4	5	6	7
Open (to new ideas, suggestions)	1	2	3	4	5	6	7
On time	1	2	3	4	5	6	7
Dedicated	1	2	3	4	5	6	7
Insightful	1	2	3	4	5	6	7
Diverse Activities	1	2	3	4	5	6	7
Enthusiastic	1	2	3	4	5	6	7
Aware of participants needs	1	2	3	4	5	6	7
Shows how to apply ideas	1	2	3	4	5	6	7

Three Greatest Strengths

1. _____
2. _____
3. _____

Three Greatest Needs

1. _____
2. _____
3. _____

Figure 13.1 *Acrostic Analysis*

type of evaluation that is the most effective. Select the evaluation strategy likeliest to give you the information you need to reach your highest expectations.

Works Cited and Suggested Readings

Boyle, Patrick G. *Planning Better Programs.* Chapter 17. New York: McGraw-Hill, 1981

Brookfield, Stephen. *Understanding and Facilitating Adult Learning.* Chapter 11. San Francisco: Jossey-Bass, 1986

Conti, G.; and Fellenz, R. A. "Evaluation: Measurement and Discovery." In *Materials and Methods in Adult and Continuing Education,* edited by C. Klevens. Los Angeles: Klevens, 1987

Draves, William A. *How to Teach Adults.* Chapter 9. Manhattan, KS: The Learning Resources Network, 1984

Dutton, M. D.; and Seaman, Don. "Self-evaluation." In *Materials and Methods in Adult and Continuing Education,* edited by C. Klevens. Los Angeles: Klevens, 1987

Guba, Egon; and Lincoln, Yvonna S. *Effective Evaluation.* San Francisco: Jossey-Bass, 1988

Knox, Alan B. *Helping Adults Learn.* Chapters 9 and 12. San Francisco: Jossey-Bass, 1987

Pike, Robert W. *Creative Training Techniques Handbook.* Minneapolis, MN: Lakewood Books, 1989

Powers, Bob. *Instructor Excellence: Mastering the Delivery of Training.* Chapters 11 and 12. San Francisco: Jossey-Bass, 1992

Seaman, Don F.; and Fellenz, Robert A. *Effective Strategies for Teaching Adults.* Chapter 6. Columbus, OH: Merrill, 1989

Sork, Thomas. J. "The Workshop as a Unique Instructional Format." In *Designing and Implementing Effective Workshops,* edited by Thomas J. Sork. San Francisco: Jossey-Bass, 1984

14

Recap

George Gordon Byron once wrote, "I wish he would explain his explanation." This chapter tries to do just that. Much of what I have said before is restated here. I hope that these pages will serve not only as a summary and reminder of the information and strategies that make up this handbook but also as a fresh look at some by now familiar ideas.

Preparing a Workshop

Thorough preparation of a workshop will increase the likelihood that the workshop will meet the needs of the participants and flow well.

1. Identify the subject.
    Choose a topic for which you have knowledge,
        enthusiasm, and passion.
2. Analyze the participants.
    What is the background and expertise of the participants?
    What are likely to be the participants' major concerns?
    How much knowledge do the participants have about the topic?
    What do they need to know about the topic?
    Is it likely that participants have attended workshops
        similar to yours?
3. Gather necessary data.
    List topics.
    Read books, journal articles, handouts.
    Talk to specialists, professionals.
    Attend conferences, workshops.
    Gather more information than you'll be able to use—it's easier
        to eliminate content than to try to improvise.
4. Identify the critical attribute.
    What is unique and essential about your workshop?
5. Identify workshop goals and aims.
    What will participants know and be able to do as a result of attending?

What do you want to accomplish during the workshop?

What is most/least important?

6. Identify involvement and interactive strategies.

Determine techniques to motivate, gain rapport, and engage
participants in the workshop.

7. Plan a presentation sequence.

Build knowledge and skill in a sequential model:

"Grab"—introduction

"Share"—content with significant illustrations, specific incidents,
research and other evidence in support

"Make Them Believe"—closing and evaluation

Determine how best to present content and allow time for
participants to process and reflect.

8. Prepare materials and outline.

Develop the workshop packet and visuals that will be the plan for
your workshop.

9. Evaluate the workshop.

What, specifically, will be evaluated?

What method of evaluation will you use?

Mind Your P's of Planning

A look at the P's of planning provides a quick and effective checklist for workshop facilitation. Before your next workshop, consider the following:

1. Participants

_____who

_____roles represented

_____level of comprehension

_____number

_____needs relating to topic

_____comfort and relaxation levels

2. Program

_____goals and aims

_____limit scope

3. Particulars

_____date

_____time

_____refreshments

_____name tags

4. Process

_____interaction strategies

_____varied format

_____opening

_____presentation of content

_____closing

5. Pacing

_____punctual beginning and ending

_____timing of activities

_____time for formal and informal interaction

_____breaks

6. Place

_____room arrangement conducive to learning

_____ventilation, temperature

_____adult-sized furniture

_____rest rooms

7. Props

_____items needed to support learning

_____media

_____handouts for participants

Guidelines for Successful Workshops

Before the Workshop

Participant assessment

Determine number of participants.

Identify possible reasons for participants to attend workshop.

Consider audience background and experience.

Workshop planning

Incorporate instructional strategies for various learning styles.

Identify goals for the workshop.

Physical arrangements

Make sure the meeting room is comfortable, the temperature
   and lighting adjusted.

See that visuals are visible from all areas of the room.

Arrange tables and chairs appropriately.

Check all audiovisual equipment to be sure it's in working order.

During the Workshop

Be at the workshop early to greet participants.

Be available during breaks to answer questions and talk.

Have an attention-getting introduction.

Emphasize key points and give relevant examples.

Use effective visuals.

Use logical, smooth transitions.

Provide a comprehensive, easy-to-follow summary.

Give clear directions for all activities.

Repeat participants' questions so all can hear.

Move throughout the room during presentation time.

Use humor appropriately and effectively.

After the Workshop

Encourage evaluation.

Be available for individual questions and concerns.

A Review of What Facilitators Do in Workshops

Identify a topic for which you have knowledge and enthusiasm.

Assess your strengths and beliefs about your program's content. Know why you want to facilitate this workshop.

Assess your participants.

Determine your outcomes. What do you want to have happen as a result of teachers attending the workshop?

Decide on major content priorities.

Collect more information than you plan to use.

Chunk content.

Use plenty of interactive activities.

Plan your opening to create interest and expectation.

Plan your transitions.

Provide frequent review and reinforcement activities.

Communicate benefits frequently.

Plan a strategy to help participants transfer their learning.

Plan a closing to help participants remember the workshop and implement its ideas and information.

Be genuine.

The best-planned workshop can fail because the facilitator didn't take some basic steps to get the participants involved and to acknowledge their needs. The most experienced facilitators have learned these basics the hard way. In the spirit of making your journey to becoming a workshop facilitator a little easier, I share these ideas with you. Some of the suggestions appear elsewhere in the handbook, it seems useful to have them in one list for easy access.

Build upon what the participants already know, understand, believe, and want. It is imperative that you find out what your participants know about the topic, what their expectations are for the workshop, and how their professional experience relates to the workshop topic. Ideally, this would be done prior to the workshop, but at the very least it should be done during the introductory moments. Sometimes you can anticipate the participants' needs because they selected the particular workshop to attend, but provide some way of checking your assumptions before the workshop progresses very far.

Have personal contact with the participants. Arrive early, make yourself available at breaks, come back early after lunch, and stay after the session to answer individual questions and chat informally with the participants. Let the participants know that you are human by interacting with them on a personal level whenever possible.

Involve the participants. Encourage the participants to think, apply, interact, and move around throughout the workshop. Challenge them to become actively involved and consciously identify what they are learning.

Share several specific examples. Remind the participants consistently and continually how the content relates to them and how they can apply what is being shared. To reinforce your point, share your personal and student examples and tell what other teachers have done with the ideas.

Acknowledge and reinforce input from the participants. When someone shares an idea or a personal experience, give it the attention it deserves. Respond to questions with care, and seek ideas and suggestions from the participants.

Begin and end on time. Reward the participants who are prompt by starting on time, initially and after breaks. Begin with some interesting material that is not critical but a bonus for those who are prompt. Always end on time or a few minutes early. If you finish late, participants will be wondering when you're going to stop rather than listening to what you have to say.

Leave the participants wanting more but not feeling cheated. It isn't always necessary for everyone to complete every activity during the workshop; it is more important that the teachers have a sense of how to do the activity. When participants leave wishing the workshop had been longer, it is likely that they are enthused about the topic and may well continue studying the subject.

Learn the names of participants whenever possible. Personalize the workshop by learning the participants' names and something about them. If the participants are wearing name tags, be sure to get close enough to be able to read their names when you are talking with them.

Test new material before using it in a workshop. Ask a colleague or several friends to preview the printed materials to be certain that the handouts communicate what you intend. Try new activities and strategies with associates before using them with strangers.

Provide incentives. Teachers, like everyone, like to be rewarded for time spent. Give away prizes such as posters, small items to be used in the classroom, or books. When appropriate, and for a longer workshop, consider presenting certificates.

Have refreshments available. Food tends to make everyone feel better. People have different periods of sugar highs and lows, and even a small piece of candy can help them through a down time. Pay special attention to some sort of food break in the afternoon.

Address problems quietly without a workshop proclamation. When the workshop facilitator mentions a problem, it becomes a problem for everyone. If someone is concerned about the temperature or lighting, for example, solve the trouble for the individual rather than bringing it up before the entire group. Once it is identified, the problem will belong to everyone, even those who had not considered it as such earlier.

Radiate energy. As the workshop facilitator, you need to have more energy than everyone else. Use diversity, movement, and humor to maintain everyone's energy. Save something that always works for those times when the workshop seems to be dragging. If all else fails, take a break.

APPENDIX

And thick and fast they came at last.
And more, and more, and more.
—Lewis Carroll

Forms, charts, and lists for your use are included here. All may be reproduced and adapted for your own workshop needs.

★ ★ ★ ★ ★

Participant Information Checklist

Check out this information regarding the participants before you begin planning your workshop.

Grade level and subject specialty:

Number:

Expertise with topic:

Special information:

Special concerns related to the topic:

Constraints:

Reason for attending the workshop:

KWL Strategy

Referring to the topic of the workshop, write appropriate responses in each of the columns below.

What I **K**now   What I **W**ant to Know   What I **L**earned

People Bingo

I have two adult children.	I am an only child.	I have at least one living parent.	I have taught more than fifteen years.	I have taught in the same school more than five years.
I have traveled to more than three foreign countries.	I live in the town where I was born.	I have multiple births in my family.	My house is more than fifty years old.	I have more than one pet at home.
I have more than one pet in my classroom.	I have taught in more than five schools.	I have lived in more than five cities as an adult.	I am teaching the same grade I taught when I began teaching.	Teaching is my second career.
I have facilitated workshops for teachers.	I am currently reading a book for pleasure.	I don't like chocolate.	This is my first year in my current position.	I have duty this week.
I have two brothers.	I had eight hours of sleep last night.	I have a baby less than a year old at home.	My favorite color is red.	My eyes are two different colors.

Facilitator Self-Evaluation:
Stars and Questions

Title of Workshop:

Date: Location:

Number of Participants:

 These ideas/activities worked well:

 Consider changing or eliminating these ideas/activities:

Learning Log Form

Ideas I will use from today's session:

How I will use the ideas:

What I will need to do before I can use the ideas:

Workshop Evaluation

Title of workshop:

Date:

What significant ideas have you learned today?

What concerns should you mention to the facilitator?

Suggestions:

Any other comments you would like to make:

Workshop Evaluation

Title of workshop:

Date:

Please respond to the statements below by circling the appropriate number code in the righthand column. The response code is

5 Strongly agree
4 Agree
3 Agree with reservations
2 Disagree
1 Strongly disagree

1. This session met my expectations.   5   4   3   2   1

2. This session will be of value to me in my current assignment. 5   4   3   2   1

3. This session will be of value to me in the future.   5   4   3   2   1

4. The physical facilities were satisfactory.   5   4   3   2   1

5. The session had clearly identifiable goals or objectives.   5   4   3   2   1

6. The session had appropriate goals or objectives.   5   4   3   2   1

7. The facilitator was knowledgeable about the topic presented. 5   4   3   2   1

8. The session had enough variety to maintain my interest.   5   4   3   2   1

9. I would recommend this workshop to a colleague.   5   4   3   2   1

10. To what extent do you agree that a more intensive follow-up 5   4   3   2   1
     to this session be scheduled.

11. What changes would you suggest if this workshop were offered again?

_____

_____

_____

Annotated Bibliography

—

Poetry and Books for Workshops

Following are some favorite books and poems to excerpt or read in their entirety during a workshop. These books and poems have been selected because they are related to learning and teaching and can be integrated with the topic of your workshop.

Annabelle Swift, Kindergartner by Amy Schwartz. Orchard, 1988. Despite her sister's instructions, Annabelle's first day at school is a success.

The Baby Uggs Are Hatching by Jack Prelutsky. Illustrated by James Stevenson. Greenwillow, 1982. Share the poem, "The Creature in the Classroom" for a guaranteed laugh.

The Blood-and-Thunder Adventure on Hurricane Peak by Margaret Mahy. McElderry, 1989. The motto of this school is "Expect the Unexpected."

The Burning Questions of Bingo Brown by Betsy Byars. Viking, 1988. Bingo tries to understand his life with the help of his school journal.

Chrysanthemum by Kevin Henkes. Greenwillow, 1991. She loves her name . . . until she goes to school.

Class Clown by Johanna Hurwitz. Morrow, 1987. Lucas Cott doesn't mean to be the class clown . . . it just happens.

Class Dismissed! by Mel Glenn. Photos by Michael J. Bernstein. Clarion, 1982. Original poems about the emotional lives of high school students.

Double Dog Dare by Jamie Gilson. Lothrop, 1988. Hobie is not in TAG, but his test shows he's the smartest.

Good Books, Good Times by edited by Lee Bennett Hopkins. Illustrated by Harvey Stevenson. Harper, 1990. A collection of poems in celebration of books.

Hey World, Here I Am! by Jean Little. Harper, 1986. The world of friendship, school, and family life according to Kate Bloomfield.

If You're Not Here, Please Raise Your Hand by Kalli Dakos. Illustrated by G. Brian Karas. Four Winds, 1990. Elementary school is celebrated in thirty-eight poems written by a teacher.

It Happens to Everyone by Bernice Myers. Lothrop, 1990. The first day of school is a little bit scary for everyone .

John Patrick Norman McHennessey: The Boy Who Was Always Late by John Burningham. Crown, 1987. His teacher isn't very understanding until . . .

*picture books

Matilda by Roald Dahl. Illustrated by Quentin Blake. Viking, 1988. Matilda is a genius —her family doesn't understand, but her kindergarten teacher sees the truth.

*Michael by Tony Bradman. Illustrated by Tony Ross. Macmillan, 1991. Einstein-like Michael just doesn't fit in, and he drives the teachers crazy.

**My Great Aunt Arizona* by Gloria Houston. HarperCollins, 1992. A thank-you to the teachers who enrich the lives of their students in so many ways.

**Never Spit on Your Shoes* by Denys Cazet. Orchard, 1990. The first day of first grade is memorable . . . for everyone!

Preposterous selected by Paul B. Janeczko. Orchard, 1991. An anthology of poems about being a teenager.

**The Principal's New Clothes* by Stephanie Calmenson. Illustrated by Denise Brunkus. Scholastic, 1989. A variation of Andersen's story about the "clothes horse" Emperor in a school setting.

Something Big Has Been Here by Jack Prelutsky. Illustrated by James Stevenson. Greenwillow, 1990. Several of these poems relate to the events that happen in school. Also: *The New Kid on the Block.* 1984

A Teacher on Roller Skates and Other School Riddles by David A. Adler. Illustrated by John Wallner. Holiday, 1989. Original and tried riddles about school.